T0212962

# Lecture Notes in Computer Science    10166

*Commenced Publication in 1973*
Founding and Former Series Editors:
Gerhard Goos, Juris Hartmanis, and Jan van Leeuwen

Nora Cuppens-Boulahia · Costas Lambrinoudakis
Frédéric Cuppens · Sokratis Katsikas (Eds.)

# Security of Industrial Control Systems and Cyber-Physical Systems

Second International Workshop, CyberICPS 2016
Heraklion, Crete, Greece, September 26–30, 2016
Revised Selected Papers

 Springer

*Editors*

Nora Cuppens-Boulahia
Telecom Bretagne
Cesson Sevigne
France

Frédéric Cuppens
Telecom Bretagne
Cesson Sevigne
France

Costas Lambrinoudakis
University of Piraeus
Piraeus
Greece

Sokratis Katsikas
Norwegian University of Science
  and Technology
Gjøvik
Norway

ISSN 0302-9743          ISSN 1611-3349   (electronic)
Lecture Notes in Computer Science
ISBN 978-3-319-61436-6          ISBN 978-3-319-61437-3   (eBook)
DOI 10.1007/978-3-319-61437-3

Library of Congress Control Number: 2017943078

LNCS Sublibrary: SL4 – Security and Cryptology

Printed on acid-free paper

This Springer imprint is published by Springer Nature
The registered company is Springer International Publishing AG
The registered company address is: Gewerbestrasse 11, 6330 Cham, Switzerland

# Preface

This book presents the revised and selected papers of the Second Workshop on the Security of Industrial Control Systems and Cyber-Physical Systems (CyberICPS 2016), held in Crete, Greece, during September 26–30, 2016, and co-located with the 21st European Symposium on Research in Computer Security (ESORICS 2016).

The event aims to address the increasing number of cyber threats that cyber-physical systems operators around the world face. Cyber-physical systems range in size, complexity, and criticality, from embedded systems used in smart vehicles, to SCADA and industrial control systems like energy and water distribution systems, smart transportation systems etc.

The workshop program included two invited papers and five full papers. The invited papers were entitled "Security of Cyber-Physical Systems: From Theory to Testbeds and Validation" and "Critical Infrastructure Protection: A Holistic Methodology for Greece" presented by Joaquin Garcia-Alfaro (Telecom SudParis, CNRS, Université Paris-Saclay, Evry, France) and George Stergiopoulos (Information Security & Critical Infrastructure Protection Laboratory, Department of Informatics, Athens University of Economics & Business, Greece), respectively. The reviewed paper sessions covered topics related to the management of cyber-security in industrial control systems and cyber-physical systems, including security monitoring, trust management, security policies and measures.

We would like to express our thanks to the people who assisted us in organizing the event and formulating the program. We are very grateful to the Program Committee members for their timely and rigorous reviews of the papers. Finally, we would like to thank all authors who submitted papers for the event and contributed to an interesting set of conference proceedings.

March 2017

Nora Cuppens-Boulahia
Costas Lambrinoudakis
Frédéric Cuppens
Sokratis Katsikas

# Organization

## General Chairs

Frédéric Cuppens     Télécom Bretagne, France
Sokratis Katsikas     Center for Cyber and Information Security, Norwegian
                     University of Science and Technology, Norway

## Program Committee Co-chairs

Nora Cuppens-Boulahia     Télécom Bretagne, France
Costas Lambrinoudakis     University of Piraeus, Greece

## Program Committee

| | |
|---|---|
| Alcaraz Cristina | University of Malaga, Spain |
| Ayed Samiha | IMT-Telecom-Bretagne, France |
| Conti Mauro | University of Padua, Italy |
| Debar Hervé | Télécom SudParis, France |
| Debbabi Mourad | Concordia University, Canada |
| Espes David | University of Brest, France |
| Gollmann Dieter | Hamburg University of Technology, Germany |
| Kanoun Waël | Alcatel-Lucent Bell Labs, France |
| Mambo Masahiro | Kanazawa University, Japan |
| Mauw Sjouke | University of Luxembourg, Luxembourg |
| Meng Weizhi | Institute for Infocomm Research, Singapore |
| Mitchell Chris | Royal Holloway, University of London, UK |
| Röning Juha | University of Oulu, Finland |
| Roudier Yves | EURECOM, France |
| Vyskoc Jozef | VaF, Slovakia |
| Wahid Khan Ferdous | Airbus Defence and Space GmbH, Germany |
| Wolthusen Stephen | Royal Holloway, University of London, UK |
| Zanero Stefano | Politecnico di Milano, Italy |

# Contents

# Invited Papers

# Security of Cyber-Physical Systems
## From Theory to Testbeds and Validation

Jose Rubio-Hernan, Juan Rodolfo-Mejias, and Joaquin Garcia-Alfaro[✉]

SAMOVAR, Telecom SudParis, CNRS, Université Paris-Saclay, Evry, France
{jose.rubio_hernan,juan.mejia_rojas,
joaquin.garcia_alfaro}@telecom-sudparis.eu

**Abstract.** Traditional control environments connected to physical systems are being upgraded with novel information and communication technologies. The resulting systems need to be adequately protected. Experimental testbeds are crucial for the study and analysis of ongoing threats against those resulting cyber-physical systems. The research presented in this paper discusses some actions towards the development of a replicable and affordable cyber-physical testbed for training and research. The architecture of the testbed is based on real-world components, and emulates cyber-physical scenarios commanded by SCADA (Supervisory Control And Data Acquisition) technologies. We focus on two representative protocols, Modbus and DNP3. The paper reports as well the development of some adversarial scenarios, in order to evaluate the testbed under cyber-physical threat situations. Some detection strategies are evaluated using our proposed testbed.

## 1 Introduction

Traditional control systems are evolving in an effort to reduce complexity and cost. These systems are converging into using a shared network layer, enabling interconnectivity between different manufacturers. Despite all the evident advantages of joining the communication layer in a shared network, this evolution also opens the door to the emergence of sophisticated cyber-threats [6,13]. These threats need to be assessed to offer novel countermeasures to minimize the risk when using shared communication layers.

Critical services infrastructures, such as water management, transportation of electricity, rail and air traffic control, belong to systems nowadays coined as Cyber-Physical Systems (CPSs). The impact of any security breach to these environments can affect the physical integrity of individuals in contact to those systems. Even basic threats such as replay cyber-physical attacks [22] could potentially cause significant damages if attack detection is not properly undertaken. Within this scope, our goal is to put in practice solutions of theoretical nature, modeled and implemented under realistic scenarios, in order to analyze their effectiveness against intentional attacks. More precisely, we assume cyber-physical environments operated by SCADA (Supervisory Control And Data Acquisition) technologies and industrial control protocols. We focus on two representative protocols, which are widely used in the industry: Modbus

© Springer International Publishing AG 2017
N. Cuppens-Boulahia et al. (Eds.): CyberICPS 2016, LNCS 10166, pp. 3–18, 2017.
DOI: 10.1007/978-3-319-61437-3_1

and DNP3 [5, 16]. Both protocols have TCP enabled versions. This allows us the emulation of cyber-physical environments under shared network infrastructures. We assume a Master-Slave design pattern, which mainly dictates that slaves would not initiate any communication unless a given master requests an initial operation. One of our objectives has been to combine these two protocols, both to allow the flexibility and support of several devices with Modbus as well as the security enhancements that DNP3 could provide as one of its features. Furthermore, some cyber-physical detection mechanisms based on challenge-response strategies proposed in [15, 20] are embedded in our SCADA testbed to experiment and analyze with their real-world performance. To complement the testbed, a set of adversarial scenarios are designed and developed to test attacks against the emulated environment. These scenarios focus on attacking the Modbus segments of the SCADA architecture. The final goal is to analyze the effectiveness of novel security methods implemented upon the emulated environment, and under the enforcement of some attack models.

**Paper Organization** — Section 2 provides the background. Section 3 provides details about the testbed implementation. Section 4 presents some experimental results. Section 5 provides related work. Section 6 concludes the paper.

## 2   Background

### 2.1   SCADA Technologies

We assume Cyber-Physical Systems operated by SCADA technologies and Industrial Control Protocols. SCADA (Supervisory Control And Data Acquisition) technologies are composed of well-defined types of field devices, such as: (1) Master Terminal Units (MTUs) and Human Machine Interfaces (HMIs), located at the topmost layer and managing device communications; (2) Remote Terminal Units (RTUs) and Programmable Logic Controllers (PLCs), controlling and acquiring data from remote equipment and connecting with the master stations; and (3) sensors and actuators.

The MTUs of a SCADA system are located at the control center of the organization. The MTUs give access to the management of communications, data storage, and control of sensors and actuators connected to RTUs. The interface to the administrators is provided via the HMIs. The RTUs are stand-alone data acquisition and control units. Their tasks are twofold: (1) to control and acquire data from process equipment (at the remote sites); and (2) to communicate the collected data to a master (supervision) station. Modern RTUs may also communicate between them (either via wired or wireless networks). The PLCs are small industrial microprocessor-based computers. The significant differences with respect to an RTU are in size and capability. Sensors are monitoring devices responsible for retrieving measurements related to specific physical phenomena, and communicate such measurements to the controllers. Actuators translate control signals to actions that are needed to correct the dynamics of the system, via the RTUs and PLCs.

## 2.2   Industrial Control Protocols

Protocols for industrial control systems built upon SCADA technologies must cover regulation rules such as delays and faults [2]. However, few protocols imposed by industrial standards provide security features in the traditional ICT security sense. Details about two representative SCADA protocols used in our work follow.

**Modbus** — One of the first protocols that stands out when working with data acquisition systems is Modbus [16]. It was developed around the 80's and it was done with no security concerns as was common at that time. It was developed by Modicon to be used with their PLCs. The protocol was formulated as a method to transmit data between electrical devices over serial lines. In the standard working mode, Modbus has a master and slave architecture, something really common for half duplex communications. The protocol is free and open source, making it really popular among the automation industry. The protocol evolved to allow different communication technologies. For instance, Modbus ASCII, for serial communications; and Modbus TCP/IP for Ethernet networks.

**Distributed Network Protocol (DNP3)** — As with Modbus, DNP3 is a query-response protocol for process automation systems. Messages are sent over serial bus connections or Ethernet networks (using the TCP/IP stack) [5]. The protocol recently has been leaning towards a more security-oriented design. Previous versions of the protocol suffered from the same kind of design conception where security was not taken into account, due to the inherent level of security that dedicated networks provided by this protocol.

## 2.3   Control-Theoretic Protection

Cyber-physical systems operated by SCADA technologies and industrial control protocols can be represented as closed-loop systems. Such systems follow closely the pattern of controlling the system based on the feedback they are getting from measurements. Several control-theoretic solutions have been presented in the literature to detect attacks against cyber-physical systems. In [24], some techniques are presented to improve the security of networked control systems using control theory. A proper example is the use of *authentication watermarks*. Stationary watermarks, i.e., Gaussian zero-mean distributed signals, are added to the control signals, in order to identify integrity attacks against the system. The watermark-based detector can identify the effect of real distribution values, generated at the output, with regard to, e.g., replayed or injected distribution values [15]. However, adversaries with enough resources to infer the dynamics of the protected system can evade detection [20]. Indeed, there are several methods that a potential attacker can use to identify and learn the behavior of the system [1]. The goal of these techniques is to obtain a mathematical model of the system, based on eavesdropped measurements. Non-parametric system identification techniques include the use of adaptive filters, such as Finite Impulse Response (FIR) filters. Some more powerful techniques to identify complex dynamic systems include the use of autoregressive methods, such as ARX (autoregressive exogenous model) and ARMAX (autoregressive-moving-average model with exogenous inputs model) [26]. These techniques can be used by malicious adversaries, in order to estimate the parameters of the system prior executing their attacks. Improvements to address those aforementioned problems have been presented in [19,20]. The goal of the testbed presented in the following section is to validate the effectiveness of the aforementioned techniques. Data derived from the testbed is expected to complement theoretical and numeric simulations provided in previous work.

## 3    Testbed Design

### 3.1    Architecture

Closed-loop systems are systems which rely upon internally gathered information to perform, correct, change or even stop actions. This kind of systems are important in the control theory branch, known to have two-way communication, one to read data and the other to forward commands.

We can observe three important block elements: the controller, the system itself, and the sensors. The controller reads data from the sensors, computes new information and transmit new commands to the system (i.e., the system control input). The system control input is generated by the controller with the purpose of correcting the behavior of the system, under some previously established limits. The system is what we normally see as the entity under control. The sensors are the feedback link between the system and the controller. Their purpose is to quantify the output and provide the necessary information to the controller, in order to compare and, if necessary, correct the behavior of the system.

The architecture proposed for our SCADA testbed works as follows. All the aforementioned elements can be distributed across several nodes in a shared network combining DNP3 and Modbus protocols (cf. Fig. 1). Likewise, one or various elements can be embedded into a single device. From a software standpoint, the controller never connects directly to the sensors. Instead, it is integrated in the architecture as a SCADA PLC (Programmable Logic Controller) node, with eventual connections to some other intermediary nodes. Such nodes are able to translate the controller commands into SCADA (e.g., either Modbus or

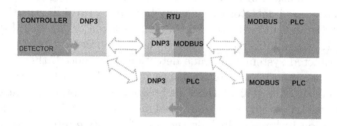

**Fig. 1.** Abstract architecture overview.

DNP3) commands. As depicted in Fig. 1, the architecture is able to handle several industrial protocols and connect to complementary SCADA elements, such as additional PLCs and RTUs (Remote Terminal Units). To evolve the architecture into a complete testbed, new elements can be included in the system, such as additional proxy-like RTU nodes.

From a data transmission standpoint, we include in our SCADA testbed the possibility of using different sampling frequencies, in order to cover a larger number of experimental scenarios. The implementation is based on control theory [19] supporting the use of different frequencies when performing read and write operations. Specifically, this narrows to the sampling frequency, a system with mono-frequency sampling is where the same frequency is used for all the channels or multi-frequency sampling where different sampling frequencies are used in each channel. Depending on the nature of the system mono or multi is better.

The architecture is able to handle many PLCs. To avoid overloading one channel with all the possible registers of the PLCs, separate ports are designated in order to isolate the communication between separated PLCs. DNP3 commands perform an Integrity Scan which gathers all the data from the PLCs in case several PLCs were being handled in the same channel, all variables of the a PLC would be fetched causing overhead in the communication.

## 3.2    Implementation Design

The implementation of our SCADA testbed consists on *Lego Mindstorms* EV3 bricks [18] and Raspberry Pi [12] boards as PLCs to control some representative sensors (e.g., distance sensors) and actuators (e.g., speed actuators). We refer the reader to http://j.mp/legoscada for additional information. Figure 2 shows an object-oriented representation of the testbed implementation, along with connection control classes, exception classes and also graphical interface classes at the controller side. In Fig. 3, we can see all the classes that have been created in order to achieve the DNP3-Modbus combination, at the RTU side. A proxy-like behavior has been also implemented allowing to translate the commands in both directions for both protocols.

**Controller Design** — The controller has a graphical interface to show the behavior of the system to an operator. It is orchestrated by the *ControlCenter* class (cf. Fig. 2). This class handles the graphical interface (cf. *HomeFrame* class) representing the HMI (Human Machine Interface) of the SCADA architecture. Some PLC instances, e.g., the *Car instances*, subsequently create DNP3 connections under a *DataHandler*, which is in charge of managing the communications between RTUs and PLCs. Finally, some of the instances (e.g., the *Car instance*) implement a graphical component to provide additional information to the operator.

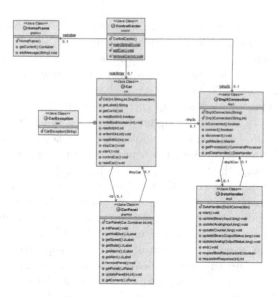

**Fig. 2.** Implementation overview, controller side.

**RTU Design** — In the implementation, it is possible to have control of one or more PLC instances. For such a task, a dedicated thread manages the translations and constant polling of each PLC. Everything starts with the *MainRTU* class (cf. Fig. 3), which opens the main DNP3 connection to expect the controller. Once the controller connects, the RTUs exchange information of the PLCs to add, and create all the respective classes in order to handle each PLC individually and with dedicated ports.

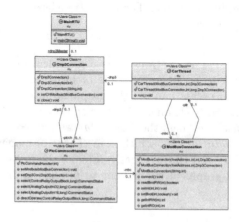

**Fig. 3.** Implementation overview, RTU side.

**External Tools** — Apart from the architecture implementation, other tools have been implemented in order to facilitate the aggregation process of new SCADA nodes. Specific custom scripts have been made to install the OpenDNP3 libraries either compiling them from source or use precompiled binaries for the case of the Raspberry Pi. Compiling source is time-consuming if it is done directly at the Raspberry Pi boards. Therefore, cross-compiling or precompiled libraries are recommended to avoid long compilation times. The Raspbian scripts give the choice to use precompiled libraries.

### 3.3 Test Scenario Description

Figure 4 shows the components of a test scenario. This scenario is a simple representation of the architecture proposed in this paper. It consists of a controller (Personal Computer), an RTU (Raspberry Pi) and a PLC (Lego EV3 Brick). The controller is always correcting the car speed and polling the distance between the car and an obstacle. One single controller and one single RTU can control various PLCs. To start the testbed is necessary to launch the Java program on the brick [23], and the intermediary Java software in the Raspberry Pi board. When starting the controller and adding a car, the controller communicates with each layer to perform the request. The car behavior is continually being modified by the controller hence varying the car speed many times per second.

### 3.4 Implementation of MiM Attacks

Man-in-the-middle (MiM) is a very common type of attack, compromising the communication in both ends, especially if the communication is not encrypted as is the case with many SCADA implementations. As mentioned previously, the watermark detectors reported in [19,20] are implemented in our testbed. Theoretical proofs and numeric simulations were already conducted to validate the proposed detectors. The testbed proposed in this paper was expected to provide complementary validation of the detectors. After having an entire architecture working, the next requirement was to implement the adversarial scenarios reported in [19,20].

In order to develop the scenarios, an attacker model was used as a base for assumptions to define the opponents' capabilities. We assume that the attacker

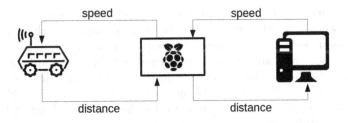

**Fig. 4.** Test scenario overview (cf. http://j.mp/legoscada).

can intercept all communication between ends, and thus the attacker can alter, store, analyze replay and forge false data in the communication. Since this is done using a testbed instead of numeric simulations, all real-life limitations are applied to the attacker. ARP poisoning [17] is used by the attacker to intercept the channels and eavesdrop the communications. The attacker has a passive and active mode of operation. The *passive mode* is where the attacker only eavesdrops, processes, and analyzes the data without modifying the information contained in the payload of the messages. Nevertheless, Ethernet header data, such as the hardware addresses, are modified since ARP tables are poisoned. During the *active mode*, the attacker starts injecting data to the hijacked communication. This injection, depending on the pattern of the attacker, can be a generated response or replayed packets.

**Replay Attack** — The attacker uses ARP poisoning to start eavesdropping the connection (passive mode). After capturing enough data, the *active mode* starts. The attacker injects the old captured data following the stream of packets of the previous capture. Before starting to disrupt the system, the attacker conducts the attack between the sensors and the controller, forging only the TCP headers that correspond to the opened TCP sessions. Once replayed the packets, the system gets disrupted by forging data between the controller and the PLCs.

**Injection Attacks** — Prior to starting the attacks, the attacker eavesdrops connections using the *passive mode*, and analyze the data in order to infer the dynamics of the system. This is used to evade the authentication watermark detector. Once inferred the model of the system, the attacker starts injecting correct data in the communication in order to defeat the watermark countermeasure. To delude the detector, the attacker calculates the effect of the watermark in the system and tries to cancel the ability of the detector to sense the changes in the feedback signal. Two different techniques are implemented: (1) a non-parametric filter, called Finite Impulse Response filter (FIR), in order to implement the evasion technique presented in [20]; and (2) autoregressive methods, such as ARX and ARMAX, in order to implement the evasion technique presented in [19].

### 3.5   Attack and Fault Detection

The adaptation of a fault detector in order to detect attacks using an authentication watermark is a valid technique that has been proved to work in [15,19,20]. The aforementioned techniques have been implemented in our SCADA testbed, in order to assess and analyze their performance using real hardware components. The testbed controllers have built-in the detector with different types of watermarks (cf. Sect. 2.3). The implementation uses the *JKalman* library [4], with some light modifications to parameterize the system and detect the effect of the watermark in the system's output. The detector estimates the next output of the system and then compares it to the value returned by the system.

The process uses the $\chi^2$ detector proposed in [15]. The detector returns a metric, $g_t$, which increases rapidly when the output of the system starts to move away from the estimation. The metric is posteriorly used to generate alerts.

The $g_t$ metric is an in-code operator that quantifies the difference between the parametric model output and the actual system output. An increase of $g_t$ means that the system is not behaving or reacting to the watermark as expected. Therefore, the system is likely to be under attack. The value of $g_t$ is calculated for each iteration and compared with the values of some previous iterations. In order to discard false positives, the controller implements the validation code presented in Algorithm 1, to separate normal faults from attacks or severe failures. The algorithm alerts the operator only when real intervention is required, making the differentiation between faults, e.g., latency or inaccuracy events at the sensor; and intentional attacks. For every feedback sample, the controller analyzes $g_t$. If $g_t$ consecutively bypasses a given threshold more than *window* times, then it triggers an *alert*.

---

**Algorithm 1.** Fault and Attack Detector

---

```
1: procedure DETECTION ALGORITHM
2:      window ← detector window
3: loop:
4:      if g_t ≥ threshold then
5:          risk ← risk + 1.
6:          if risk > window then
7:              alert ← alert + 1.
8:      else
9:          risk ← 0.
```

---

## 4   Experimentation and Results

### 4.1   Experimentation

We present in this section the results of applying the watermark authentication technique presented in [19,20] under the testbed presented in Sect. 3. Several repetitions of the experiment were orchestrated using automated scripts handling the elements of our SCADA testbed scenarios. The scripts can perform several actions, such as starting the controller and the RTUs, as well as executing the predefined attacks. A set of attacks and detectors have been used and posteriorly analyzed. The combinations, attack–detector, are the following:

- *Replay Attack–Watermark Disabled:* the attacker is likely to evade the detector, since no watermark is injected into the system.
- *Replay Attack–Watermark Enabled:* the attacker is likely identified by the detector, since the attack is not able to adapt to the current watermark.

– *Non-parametric Attack–Stationary Watermark:* attacker and detector have equal chances of success.
– *Non-parametric Attack–Non-stationary Watermark:* the non-stationary watermark changes the distribution systematically, hence preventing the FIR-based attack to adapt to such changes. The expected results are an increase of the detection ratio.
– *Parametric Attack–Stationary Watermark:* the attacker is likely to evade the detector when the attack properly infers the system parameters.
– *Parametric Attack–Non-stationary Watermark:* the attacker is also likely to evade the detector when the system parameters are properly identified.

The cyber-physical implications of the testbed hinder the experimentation process especially when several repetitions are required in order to obtain statistical results, contrary to simulations where only the code is executed. The creation of the orchestration script, which automates the test, has been necessary to simplify the experimentation tasks. Next section shows the results using the testbed for the aforementioned attacker-detector combinations. A sample execution of the *Replay Attack – Watermark Disabled* scenario is available at http://j.mp/legoscada.

### 4.2   Experimental Results

After collecting data from different devices across the SCADA testbed, the data is analyzed accordingly to interpret the performance of the detector with regard to the attack scenario. Since the stationary watermark detector was correctly refined for each test scenario, we are able to analyze in depth the results through a statistical evaluation of the data. Experimental results with the non-stationary watermark mechanism are also conducted. Figure 5 shows the detector values, $g_t$, for all the attack-detector combinations defined in Sect. 4.1.

For all the plots, the solid horizontal line represents the threshold; and the vertical dotted line represents the moment when the attacker starts injecting malicious data. The short peaks on the left side of the plots, those bypassing the threshold line before the start of the attacks, are counted as false positives or system faults.

Figures 5(a) and (b) show the experimental results of the replay attack. When the watermark was disabled (cf. Fig. 5(a)), the attacker properly evades the detector. Since the controller is not inserting the protection watermark, it does not detect the attack. On the contrary, the results in Fig. 5(b) show that the activation of the watermark under the same scenario allows the controller to alert about the attack almost immediately. Based on these results, we can conclude that the stationary watermark based detector properly works out to detect the replay attack.

Figure 5(c) represents the non-parametric attacker against the previously tested stationary watermark. The detector is now unable to detect the attacker. Figure 5(d) shows the case where the non-stationary watermark is enabled. Under this situation, the detector has lightly more chances of detecting the

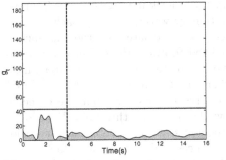

(a) No watermark under replay attack

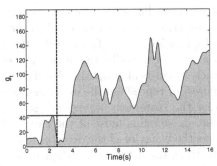

(b) Stationary watermark under replay attack

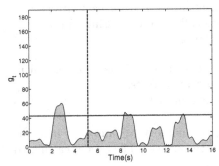

(c) Stationary watermark under non-parametric attack

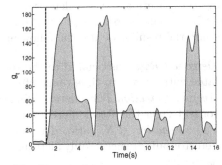

(d) Non-stationary watermark under non-parametric attack

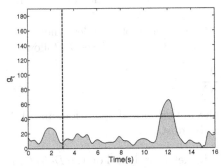

(e) Stationary watermark under parametric attack

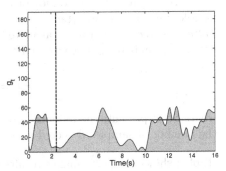

(f) Non-stationary watermark under parametric attack

**Fig. 5.** Detection results. The horizontal solid line represents the threshold. The vertical dotted line represents the moment when the attack starts. Peaks on the left side of the vertical dotted line represent false positives. (a), (b) detection values of $g_t$, without and with stationary watermark under replay attack. (c), (d) detection values with stationary and non-stationary watermark under non-parametric attack. And (e), (f) detection values with stationary and non-stationary watermark under parametric attack.

attack. This shows how the non-stationary watermark mechanism does improve the detection abilities compared to the stationary watermark approach.

Figures 5(e) and (f) evaluate the scenario associated to the parametric attacks. Theoretically, the attacker is expected to evade the detector when the attack succeeds at properly identifying the parameters of the system dynamics. Figure 5(e) represents the experiments where the parametric attack is executed under the stationary watermark scenario. The figure shows that the detector value, $g_t$, remains most of the time below the detection threshold. Figure 5(f) shows the behavior of the detector under the non-stationary watermark scenario. This time, the detector has slightly more chances of detecting the attack.

### 4.3   Statistical Data Evaluation

Using the watermark-based detection mechanism, we run for each attack scenario 75 automated rounds (about 4 h of data collection processing). In order to evaluate the results, we use the following metrics:

1. *Detection Ratio*, associated to the success percentage of the detector, calculated with regard to time range after each attack starts.
2. *Average Detection Time*, determining the amount of time needed by the detector to trigger the attack alert.
3. *False Negative (FN)* ratio, determining the number of samples where the detector fails at successfully alerting about the attacks. The ratio is calculated as follows,

$$FN = \frac{SA - AD}{SA} \tag{1}$$

where $SA$ represents the values of the samples under attack, and $AD$ the samples detected as an attack.

4. *False Positives (FP)* ratio, calculated as the number of samples where the detector signals benign events as attacks. The ratio is calculated as follows,

$$FP = \frac{AD}{SN} \tag{2}$$

where $SN$ represents the number of samples under normal operation, and $AD$ the number of samples detected as attack by mistake.

Table 1 shows the performance results of the detector, based on the *Detection Ratio* and the *Average detection Time* metrics.

**Table 1.** Detector performance results.

|  | Replay attack | Non-parametric attack | Parametric attack |
|---|---|---|---|
| *Detection Ratio* | 40.00% | 18.00% | 12.00% |
| *Average Detection Time* | 18.81 s | 10.17 s | 6.08 s |

Regarding the results shown in Table 1, we can emphasize that the replay attack is the most detectable scenario, with a detection ratio of about 40%. This detection ratio is still far from perfect, maybe due to the sensors accuracy and resolution; but better than for the rest of scenarios. The non-parametric attacker has a lower detection ratio, of about 18%. This result is expected, as suggested by the theoretical and simulation-based conclusions available at [20], where the authors emphasize that the mechanism is not sufficiently robust to detect adversaries that are able to identify the system model. To finish, the parametric attack has the most robust system identification approach. The attacks can evade the detection process if they succeed at properly identifying the system attributes. In terms of results, they lead to the lowest detection rate of about 12%.

During the replay attack, the *Average Detection Time* is the slowest of all the adversarial scenarios. This behavior is due to the watermark distribution properties, since the watermark variation makes the replay attack highly detectable. At the same time, the injection attacks (either the parametric or the non-parametric version) are detected much faster than the replay attack. This is due to the transition period needed by the attackers to estimate the correct data prior misleading the detector. For this reason, if the attacker does not choose the precise moment to start the attack, the detector implemented at the controller side is able to detect the injected data, right at the beginning of the attack. Furthermore, the attackers shall also synchronize their estimations to the measurements sent by the sensors. In case of failing the synchronization process, the detector does identify the uncorrelated data, and reports the attack.

Table 2 shows that the detection of the replay attack has the lowest false negative ratio, 64.06%, hence confirming that this adversarial scenario is the most detectable situation with regard to the detection techniques reported in [15]. The detection of the non-parametric attacks has a higher false negative ratio, 85.20%, confirming the theoretical and simulation-based results reported in [20]. The detection of the parametric attacks also confirms the results estimated in [19], and leading to the highest false negative ratio, 88.63%. Finally, and in terms of false positive ratio, the three adversarial scenarios show a low impact (on average, about 1.33% false positive ratio). Such low impact is, moreover, easy to tune by adapting the parameters of Algorithm 1.

## 5   Related Work

The study of security incidents associated to cyber-physical systems underlying critical infrastructures has gathered a big amount of attention since the infamous

**Table 2.** Long run experiment results.

|                 | Replay attack | Non-parametric attack | Parametric attack |
|-----------------|---------------|-----------------------|-------------------|
| *False Negatives* | 64.06%        | 85.20%                | 88.63%            |
| *False Positives* | 0.98%         | 1.66%                 | 1.35%             |

Stuxnet case [13]. Since then, research on cyber-physical systems has progressed substantially resulting in a large number of testbeds developed and established in the literature. A non-exhaustive list follows.

Myat-Aung present in [9] a Secure Water Treatment (SWaT) simulation and testbed to test defense mechanisms against a variety of attacks. Siaterlis et al. [21] define a cyber-physical Experimentation Platform for Internet Contingencies (EPIC) that is able to study multiple independent infrastructures and to provide information about the propagation of faults and disruptions. Green et al. [7] focus their work on an adaptive cyber-physical testbed where they include different equipments, diverse networks, and also business processes. Yardley reports in [25] a cyber-physical testbed based on commercial tools in order to experimentally validate emerging research and technologies. The testbed combines emulation, simulation, and real hardware to experiment with smart grid technologies. Krotofil and Larsen show in [11] several testbeds and simulations concluding that a successful attack against their envisioned systems has to manage cyber and physical knowledge.

From a more control-theoretic standpoint, Candell et al. report in [3] a testbed to analyze the performance of security mechanisms for cyber-physical systems. The work reports as well discussions from control and security practitioners. McLaughlin et al. analyze in [14] different testbeds and conclude that it is necessary to use pathways between cyber and physical components of the system in order to detect attacks. Also, Koutsandria et al. [10] implement a testbed where the data are cross-checked, using cyber and physical elements. Holm et al. survey, classify and analyze in [8] several cyber-physical testbeds proposed for scientific research. Inline with the aforementioned contributions, we have presented in this paper an ongoing testbed that aims at evaluating research mitigation techniques targeting attacks at the physical layer of cyber-physical systems operated via SCADA protocols. The initial focus of our testbed has been the evaluation of the control-theoretic security mechanisms reported in [15, 19, 20].

## 6    Conclusion

In pursuance of security testing in cyber-physical systems, this paper has provided a practical description of an ongoing platform to test theoretical cyber-physical defense techniques. The architecture of the testbed is based on real-world components, in order to emulate cyber-physical systems commanded by SCADA (Supervisory Control And Data Acquisition) technologies. Two real-world protocol implementations are included within our platform.

Three types of adversarial scenarios were also integrated in our testbed. The three scenarios enforce different types of attackers, incrementing the usability of the testbed to experiment novel security methods against a wider variety of malicious intents. All three scenarios were confronted against representative defense techniques. The platform also implements testing automation in order to provide larger datasets as results and enabling the architecture to perform repetitive tests. Experimental results confirm previous theoretical and simulation-based work.

**Acknowledgements.** The authors acknowledge support from the Cyber CNI Chair of Institut Mines-Télécom. The chair is held by Télécom Bretagne and supported by Airbus Defence and Space, Amossys, EDF, Orange, La Poste, Nokia, Société Générale and the Regional Council of Brittany. It has been acknowledged by the Center of excellence in Cybersecurity.

# References

1. Aarts, R.: System identification and parameter estimation. Technical report, Faculty of Engineering Technology, University Twente (2012)
2. Brown, S.: Overview of IEC 61508 design of electrical/electronic/programmable electronic safety-related systems. Comput. Control Eng. J. **11**(1), 6–12 (2000)
3. Candell, R., Stouffer, K., Anand, D.: A cybersecurity testbed for industrial control systems. In: Process Control and Safety Symposium International Society of Automation, Houston, TX (2014)
4. Chmelar, P.: Java kalman library (2014). https://sourceforge.net/projects/jkalman/. Accessed Oct 2016
5. Curtis, K.: A DNP3 protocol primer. A basic technical overview of the protocol (2005). http://www.dnp.org/AboutUs/DNP3%20Primer%20Rev%20A.pdf. Accessed Oct 2016
6. Graham, J.H., Patel, S.C.: Security considerations in SCADA communication protocols. Technical report TR-ISRL-04-01 (2004). http://www.cs.louisville.edu/facilities/ISLab/tech%20papers/ISRL-04-01.pdf. Accessed Oct 2016
7. Green, B., Hutchison, D., Frey, S.A.F., Rashid, A.: Testbed diversity as a fundamental principle for effective ICS security research. In: Proceedings of the First International Workshop on Security and Resilience of Cyber-Physical Infrastructures (SERECIN). Lancaster University, Technical report SCC-2016-01, pp. 12–15 (2016)
8. Holm, H., Karresand, M., Vidström, A., Westring, E.: A survey of industrial control system testbeds. In: Buchegger, S., Dam, M. (eds.) Secure IT Systems. LNCS, vol. 9417, pp. 11–26. Springer, Cham (2015). doi:10.1007/978-3-319-26502-5_2
9. Kaung Myat, A.: Secure Water Treatment Testbed (SWaT): an overview (2015). https://itrust.sutd.edu.sg/wp-content/uploads/sites/3/2015/11/Brief-Introduction-to-SWaT_181115.pdf. Accessed Oct 2016
10. Koutsandria, G., Gentz, R., Jamei, M., Scaglione, A., Peisert, S., McParland, C.: A real-time testbed environment for cyber-physical security on the power grid. In: 1st ACM Workshop on Cyber-Physical Systems-Security and/or Privacy, pp. 67–78. ACM (2015)
11. Krotofil, M., Larsen, J.: Rocking the pocket book: Hacking chemical plants for competition and extortion. DEF CON **23** (2015)
12. Lagu, S.S., Deshmukh, S.B.: Raspberry Pi for automation of water treatment plant. In: International Conference on Computing Communication Control and Automation (ICCUBEA), pp. 532–536, February 2015
13. Langner, R.: Stuxnet: dissecting a cyberwarfare weapon. IEEE Secur. Priv. **9**(3), 49–51 (2011)

14. McLaughlin, S., Konstantinou, C., Wang, X., Davi, L., Sadeghi, A.-R., Maniatakos, M., Karri, R.: The cybersecurity landscape in industrial control systems. Proc. IEEE **104**(5), 1039–1057 (2016)

15. Mo, Y., Weerakkody, S., Sinopoli, B.: Physical authentication of control systems: designing watermarked control inputs to detect counterfeit sensor outputs. IEEE Control Syst. **35**(1), 93–109 (2015)

16. Modbus Organization. Official Modbus Specifications (2016). http://www.modbus.org/specs.php. Accessed Oct. 2016

17. Nam, S.Y., Kim, D., Kim, J.: Enhanced ARP: preventing ARP poisoning-based man-in-the-middle attacks. IEEE Commun. Lett. **14**(2), 187–189 (2010)

18. Rollins, M.: Beginning LEGO MINDSTORMS EV3. Apress, Berkeley (2014)

19. Rubio-Hernan, Jose, Cicco, Luca, Garcia-Alfaro, Joaquin: Event-triggered watermarking control to handle cyber-physical integrity attacks. In: Brumley, Billy Bob, Röning, Juha (eds.) NordSec 2016. LNCS, vol. 10014, pp. 3–19. Springer, Cham (2016). doi:10.1007/978-3-319-47560-8_1

20. Rubio-Hernan, J., De Cicco, L., Garcia-Alfaro, J., Revisiting a watermark-based detection scheme to handle cyber-physical attacks. In: 11th International Conference on Availability, Reliability and Security, Salzburg, Austria. IEEE, September 2016

21. Siaterlis, C., Genge, B., Hohenadel, M.: EPIC: a testbed for scientifically rigorous cyber-physical security experimentation. IEEE Trans. Emerg. Topics Comput. **1**(2), 319–330 (2013)

22. Teixeira, A., Shames, I., Sandberg, H., Johansson, K.H.: A secure control framework for resource-limited adversaries. Automatica **51**, 135–148 (2015)

23. Wimberger, D., Charlton, J.: Java modbus library (2004). http://jamod.sourceforge.net. Accessed Oct 2016

24. Wu, G., Sun, J., Chen, J.: A survey on the security of cyber-physical systems. Control Theory Technol. **14**(1), 2–10 (2016)

25. Yardley, T.: Testbed cross-cutting research (2014). https://tcipg.org/research/testbed-cross-cutting-research. Accessed Oct 2016

26. Zhu, Y.: New development in industrial MPC identification. In: Proceedings of the International Symposium on Advanced Control of Chemical Processes (ADChEM), Hong Kong, China, January 2003

# Critical Infrastructure Protection:
# A Holistic Methodology for Greece

Dimitris Gritzalis[1(✉)], George Stergiopoulos[1],
Panayiotis Kotzanikolaou[2], Emmanouil Magkos[3],
and Georgia Lykou[1]

[1] Information Security and Critical Infrastructure Protection Laboratory,
Department of Informatics, Athens University of Economics and Business,
76 Patission Avenue, 10434 Athens, Greece
{dgrit,geostergiop,lykoug}@aueb.gr
[2] Department of Informatics, University of Piraeus,
85 Karaoli & Dimitriou Street, 18534 Piraeus, Greece
pkotzani@unipi.gr
[3] Department of Informatics, Ionian University,
7 Tsirigoti Square, 49100 Corfu, Greece
emagos@ionio.gr

**Abstract.** The protection of Critical Infrastructures (CI) is, by definition, of high importance for the welfare of citizens, due to direct threats (dictated by the current international political situation) and also due to their dependencies at international and European levels. Today, Greece remains one of the countries of the European Union, which has no comprehensive strategy to safeguard national CI, nor any process of developing such an integrated plan, except for some initiatives taken from the General Secretariat of Digital Policy. This paper aims to contribute to: (i) The creation of an inventory of all stakeholders, (legislative, supervisory or regulatory) involved in CI protection in Greece, (ii) the identification of potential national CI, as well as their interdependencies, (iii) the development of a structured identification based on impact assessment methodology for national CI, that takes into account internationally applied CI assessment methodologies, and (iv) provide a pilot implementation of the proposed methodology.

## 1 Introduction

The protection of Critical Infrastructures (CI) is, by definition, of high importance for the welfare of citizens of each country; especially nowadays, both because of direct threats (dictated by the current international political situation) and also due to emerging interactions or dependencies [13–15] developed between national CI at international and European levels.

Today, Greece remains one of the few countries of the European Union, which, be-sides the formal transposition of the 114/2008/EC Directive into domestic legislation, has not implemented a comprehensive CI protection strategy, nor any process of developing such an integrated plan, except for some initiatives taken by the General Secretariat of Digital Policy.

N. Cuppens-Boulahia et al. (Eds.): CyberICPS 2016, LNCS 10166, pp. 19–34, 2017.
DOI: 10.1007/978-3-319-61437-3_2

This paper presents some of the results which derived from project OLIKY[1] that aimed to provide a road-map towards the development of a holistic national CIP strategy for Greece. The basic goals of OLIKY included, among others:

1. The initial creation of an inventory and an initial ranking of candidate national CI, along with their supervised entities, in order to identify the most critical services and their dependencies, to adequately protect and increase their resilience against known or unknown threats.
2. The assessment of critical services and interdependencies between candidate national CI based on a methodology for the classification of national critical components.

The objectives of the OLIKY project did not include a comprehensive coverage and assessment of all national CI, nor the proposal of a detailed security policy for each CI. This would not be feasible in the context of an independent study, since the complete recording and evaluation of all CI nationwide requires an authorized body with the institutional and legal feasibility of collecting and processing classified information along with the cooperation of all national CI operators. However, an initial systematic identification and evaluation of Greek CI may act as a catalyst for conducting such an in-depth analysis.

**Contribution**. The main contributions of this paper include:

1. The development of an inventory of all stakeholders, (legislative, supervisory or regulatory) involved in the protection of the Greek CI.
2. The identification of potential national CI, as well as their interdependencies. In particular, an attempt was made to identify national CIs on the Energy, Transport and Information and Communication Technologies (ICT) sectors.
3. The development of a structured identification methodology for national CI, taking into account internationally applied CI identification methodologies. A range of three evaluation levels (criticality) and specific evaluation criteria for the integration of critical components in criticality levels will also be developed and utilized, as part of the proposed methodology.
4. The pilot implementation of the proposed methodology to a list of candidate national CI fields in order to rank their criticality; namely on the Energy and ICT sectors.

## 2   A Preliminary Record of Greek Critical Infrastructures

The identification and evaluation of national CI first requires the creation of an initial list of potential CI, at sector and subsector levels. In this section, the services of three key critical sectors of the country are being mapped; namely those concerning the Energy, Transport and ICT sectors.

---

[1] All OLIKY project deliverables (in Greek) can be found at: http://www.dianeosis.org/2016/07/ideas_infrastractures_protection/.

As part of a national CI protection program, each EU Member-State (MS) is re-quired to: (i) record its National Critical Areas, (ii) record and evaluate the systems or parts thereof which may constitute a CI, and (iii) to record and evaluate (possible) inter-dependencies between the identified CI. Also, each MS has to plan and/or up-date a Business Continuity Plan (BCP) and a Contingency Plan (CP) for the protection of its national CI [1–6]. Since, in most cases, the owners and/or operators of CI are private entities, any national CI identification process (along with all processes in the context of a national protection program) requires the exchange of information between stakeholders, in accordance with the principle of collaboration between stakeholders and the Public-Private Partnership (PPP) [12]. During the stage of critical area iden-tification, each MS must establish an initial list of critical national sectors, i.e. sectors existing in the geographical limits of the country that include contingent CI. Still, the process of selecting national critical sectors and sub-sectors is not obvious [2].

Towards creating a common framework program for the EPCIP (European Pro-gramme for Critical Infrastructure Protection) the establishment of a common list of critical sectors/subsectors is highly encouraged [1–6]. The concept of critical service is often used by implication instead of the term infrastructure, since it integrates the existence of a set of goods and processes that need protection and are examined in general and with detailed analysis. The list of CI is presented in Table 1 and incor-porates the concept of service per subsector.

**Table 1.** List of potential CI, sectors, and subsectors selected for Greece

| Sector | Subsector | Service |
|---|---|---|
| Energy | Electricity | Generation (all forms)/ Transmission |
| | | Distribution/Electricity market |
| | Oil | Extraction/Refinemen |
| | | Transport/Storage |
| | Natural gas | Extraction/Transport |
| | | Distribution/Storage |
| Information and communication technologies (ICT) | Information technologies | Web services/Internet |
| | | Computer networks/Services cloud |
| | | Software as a service (SaaS) |
| | Communications | Voice/Data communications |
| | | Mobile communications/Satelite |
| | | Radio communication/Broadcasting |
| Water | Drinking water | Water storage/Quality assurance |
| | | Water distribution |
| | Wastewater | Wastewater collection & treatment |

(*continued*)

**Table 1.** (*continued*)

| Sector | Subsector | Service |
|---|---|---|
| Food | Food supply chains | Agriculture/Food production |
| | | Food supply |
| | | Food distribution/Quality/Safety |
| Health | Hospital & heath facilities | Emergency healthcare/Hospital care (inpatient & outpatient) |
| | | Supply of medicines, vaccines, blood & medical supplies |
| | | Control of infections and epidemics |
| Financial services | | Banking/Stock exchange |
| | | Payment transactions |
| Public order & security | Public order | Maintenance of public order and safety |
| | Justice | Judiciary and penal systems |
| Transportations | Aviation | Air navigation services |
| | | Airport operation |
| | Road transport | Bus/Tram services/Road network maintenance |
| | Train transport | Railway network management |
| | | Railway transport services |
| | Maritime transport | Navigation control - cruises |
| | | Coastal interconnection |
| | Postal services | Logistic services |
| | | Payment transactions |
| Industry | Critical industries | Employment/GDP/Supply of goods |
| | Chemical/Nuclear industry | Storage & disposal of hazardous materials |
| | | Safety of high risk industrial units |
| | Tourism | Hotel supplies |
| | | Restaurant supplies |
| | Agriculture | Agricultural unit supply |
| | | Water supply services |
| Public administration | Government/Ministries | Government functions |
| | Regional administration | Civil services |
| Civil protection | | Emergency and rescue services |

(*continued*)

**Table 1.** (*continued*)

| Sector | Subsector | Service |
|---|---|---|
| Environment | | Air pollution monitoring and early warning |
| | | Meteorological monitoring and early warning |
| | | Ground water (lake/river) monitoring and early warning |
| | | Marine pollution monitoring and control |
| Defense | | National defense |

In order to identify candidate Greek CI, the ENISA List of Critical Sectors and Related Critical Services [7] was used to create an overview of the Critical Sectors as reported in Table 1, where specific areas were selected as being more significant for the country. Potential critical services which were irrelevant to Greek Activities (e.g. Space sector) were removed from the list due to non-conformity, while others have been added due to their potentially high impact on Greece's GDP, like Tourism and associated services.

Based on the collection of public information and scientific expertise of the panel members, the following critical areas were selected for our study: (a) Energy (b) Information and Communications Technologies (ICT) and (c) Transportation.

Results from identifying interdependencies and main stakeholders for these three fundamental CI sectors are presented in Tables 2, 3 and 4, respectively. These tables contain critical domains, sub domains for each critical service, the key subsystems that are necessary for providing each service, the essential interdependencies with other (sub) sectors, as well as an inventory of the providers of each service involved in the country.

**Energy sector**

In Greece, multiple providers support various subsectors of the Energy sector. In some subsectors, only one provider (or a very small number of them) has a dominant position, making him the obvious choice for a CI at the Energy sector. Still, some changes have occurred in the Energy market of other subsectors over the last years; usually because of Greece's need to comply with the relevant European Directives, but also due to the economic situation of the country.

**ICT sector**

The Information and Telecommunication Technologies (ICT sector) is a sector of high criticality since it provides information assets and services to almost all other critical services in the country. Of all the ICT subsectors, it appears that the Telecommunication subsector is the most important in Greece. Hardcore centralization of services is observed at the Greek ICT sector, although for some services there seems to be a more balanced distribution of providers. For this reason several providers have been identified as candidate CI for this sector although their "weight" may significantly vary.

**Table 2.** Summary of the energy sector in Greece

| Critical subsector | Critical service | Interdependencies | | Main Stakeholders |
|---|---|---|---|---|
| | | Depends upon | Affects | |
| Electricity | AC/DC production | Mining of lignite | All sectors | Public power corporation |
| | | General transfer | | Alternative electric power producers |
| | | Oil transfer | | PPC Renewables |
| | Transportation/Storage | All sectors | All sectors | Hellenic electricity distribution network operator |
| | Electrical. Energy market | Production | All sectors | Public power corporation |
| | | Distribution | | Alternative electric power producers |
| Oil | Mining | Refinement | Industry | Energean oil & gas |
| | | Transport | | |
| | | Storage | | |
| | Refinement | Transport storage | Business | Hellenic Petroleum |
| | | | | Motor Oil Hellas |
| | Transport | Shipping | Agriculture | Hellenic Petroleum |
| | | Internal relations | Transportation | Shipping Sector |
| | Storage | Oil transfer | | Motor Oil Hellas |
| | | | | Hellenic Petroleum |
| Natural Gas | Transportation/Distribution | Cross-border | Industry Domestic use | Public Gas Corp. |
| | | Interconnections | | |
| | | External relations | | TAP (under construction) |
| | Storage | Transport/Distribution | | Puplic Gas Corp. |
| | | External relations | | (LNG Revithousa) |

**Table 3.** Summary of the ICT sector in Greece

| Critical Subsector | Critical Service | Interdependencies | | Main Stakeholders |
|---|---|---|---|---|
| | | Depends upon | Affects | |
| Telecoms | Voice/Data coms | Power supply internet access external links | All sectors | OTE Group (COSMOTE, OTEGlobe, OTESAT - MARITEL, CosmoOne) Vodafone Greece WIND Hellas Forthnet CYTA |
| | Internet access | Voice/Data Communications External Links | | |
| Information technologies | Data centers/Cloud services | Power supply Providing Telecommunications Internet access Tel/Stances (ext. links) | Economy Business Industry | Med nautilus OTE Lamda Helix |
| | Web services | Power Supply providing telecoms Internet access ICT ConAbroad | Economy business | Telecommunications providers small providers |

**Table 4.** Summary of the transportation sector in greece

| Critical Subsector | Critical Service | Interdependencies | | Main Stakeholders |
|---|---|---|---|---|
| | | Depends upon | Affects | |
| Road transport | Motorways, national and provincial roads | Availability of oil ICT Systems | Provision of road transportation | Min. of infrastructure and transport technical contractors (Companies) |
| | | Interoperability infrastructure | Social & economic growth | |
| | | Environment & weather | | |
| | Provision of road passenger transport and cargo | Motorways, national and provincial Roads | Trade | National and international transport companies |
| | | Availability of oil | Government | Transport agencies |
| | | Road Signage | Business | Urban Transport: OASA, OSY, STASY |
| | | Environment & weather | Industry | OASTH |
| | | | Agriculture | Suburban buses |

*(continued)*

**Table 4.** (*continued*)

| Critical Subsector | Critical Service | Interdependencies | | Main Stakeholders |
|---|---|---|---|---|
| | | Depends upon | Affects | |
| Shipping | Ports and port infrastructure | Availability | Providing ferry transport | Min. of infrastructure and transport |
| | | ICT Systems | Trade | Min. of Shipping and Island Policy |
| | | Interoperability infrastructure | Industry | Piraeus Port Authority SA COSCO SA |
| | | Environment & weather | Enterprises | Thessaloniki port authority SA |
| | | | Agriculture | Greek port authorities |
| | Coastal transport & transportation | Port infrastructure | Tourism | Ferry operators transport companies |
| | | Availability of mineral resources & energy | Trade | Tourist companies |
| | | Marine signaling system | Industry | |
| | | ICT systems | Enterprises | |
| | | Environment & weather | Agriculture | |
| Aviation | Airports and airport infrastructure | Availability | Air transportation tourism | Hellenic civil aviation authority |
| | | ICT systems | | Athens international airport |
| | | Interoperability infrastructure | | Hellenic republic asset development fund |
| | | Environment & weather | | |
| | Air transport | Availability petroleum | Tourism Trade | Hellenic civil aviation authority |
| | | System radar air navigation services | | AIRCARRIERS |
| | | ICT Systems | Government agencies | EUROCONTROL |
| | | Environment & Weather | | |
| Rail Transport | Network Rail infrastructure | Communications systems & information | Trade industry | Greek Railways/OSE SA |
| | | | | ERGOSE SA |
| | | | | GAIAOSE SA |

(*continued*)

**Table 4.** (*continued*)

| Critical Subsector | Critical Service | Interdependencies | | Main Stakeholders |
|---|---|---|---|---|
| | | Depends upon | Affects | |
| | Rail transport | Rail infrastructure network | Trade | Greek railways companies |
| | | Energy availability | Industry | TRAINOSE SA |
| | | ICT systems | Business | STASY SA |
| | | Interoperability infrastructure | Agriculture | AMEL SA |
| | | | Tourism | TRAM SA |

**Transportation Sector**

The transport sector provides services to multiple other sectors and supports many economic activities such as trading, tourism, industry, rural development and the exploitation of natural resources of Greece. The sector is subdivided into Road, Sea, Air and Rail transport along with postal services.

# 3   Method for Determining and Evaluating National CI

This section describes a methodology for identifying and evaluating national CI, structured as a sequence of steps. Each step provides a brief description, the data (or parameters) input necessary for the execution, and implementation actions needed and expected results. The development of the methodology took into consideration previous work from other EU members [7–12, 16–20, 26], since following a best practice and creating a common baseline throughout the EU is of outmost importance.

Categories of criteria for the integration of candidate CI were defined inside the methodology. These include direct assessment criteria, time-based criteria and indirect criteria used to evaluate the "importance" of the CI. Direct evaluation criteria are based on the assessment of potential impact (impact-based classification) that are expected to manifest after an attack on relevant infrastructures.

Time-based criteria such as estimated recovery time, and estimated impact evolution over time are used for prioritizing CI within each risk level. Indirect criteria consider, amongst others, second order dependencies, which may eventually upgrade a candidate CI to a higher criticality level, e.g., when other critical elements depend on it. Indeed, the analysis of interdependencies between CI can identify CI that might have been underestimated during previous analysis [13–15, 21–25].

For each critical service sectorial and horizontal criteria are utilized for the identification of its most important subsystems. The methodology does not take into account threats (threats or scenarios), nor does it assess them according to their likelihood. A schematic overview of the described Methodology is presented in Fig. 1.

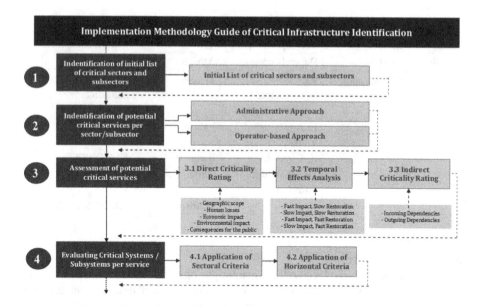

**Fig. 1.** Schematic overview of the methodology

## STEP 1: Initial list of critical sectors and subsectors

*Short description.* In the first step an initial list of potential national critical sectors and subsectors per sector is catalogued. Sectors and subsectors from the list of services offered in Table 1 are used as input.

*Implementation.* Cataloguing of the initial sectors/-subsectors list is performed by a central authority. Typically, this can be coordinated by the respective competent body for the protection of national CI.

*Results.* The initial list of critical sectors/sub-sectors will be given as input to Step 2 and Step 3.

## STEP 2: Identify potential critical services per sector/subsector

*Short description.* For each critical area, potential critical services are identified. The list compiled from Step 1 can be considered as initial parameter in the process of identifying potential critical services per sector/sub-sector, along with good-practices from EU members [9–12] which are mature enough when it comes to implementing strategies for the protection of national CI.

*Implementation.* There are two alternative approaches that can be followed to identify possible national critical services sector/subsector [7]:

*Administrative Approach.* A list of potential national critical sector services is compiled at a central, administrative level, in cooperation with a competent Authority. According to Operator-based approach, a Critical Operator list is compiled (in-line with relevant legal frameworks). Operators will be responsible to identify critical services that are involved in.

*Results.* The list of critical services sector/subsector will be given as input to Step 3 for the risk assessment of possible critical services per sub-sector.

**STEP 3: Assessment of potential critical services**

*Short description.* Possible critical elements from previous steps (sub-sector and/or services by sub-sector) are assessed and prioritized using specific criteria. Initial parameters that can be considered for the evaluation of potential critical subsectors/services are:

– The initial list of possible critical sectors/subsectors from Step 1.
– The initial list of potential critical services from Step 2 (this list may include the list from Step 1).
– The non-binding guidelines of the European Council [5] on the implementation of the horizontal criteria during the evaluation of CI.
– Good practices from EU members [12].

*Implementation.* Depending on the approach taken during Step 2 (Administrative approach or Operator-based approach), the following checks are applied, either at central level or in collaboration with Critical Administrators:

*Step 3.1. Direct criticality rating.* All potential critical services are assessed, based on the immediate consequences that would result from their breach or failure. This is achieved by applying selected horizontal criteria, from the following list [5, 6]:

– Geographic scope: The scope of the area to be affected by an event.
– Human losses: The number of victims and/or injured people.
– Economic impact: The impact in a macro and/or macro-social level.
– Environmental impact: Long-term environmental effects.
– Consequences for the public: Impact of events affecting the people, which does not directly relate to any of the previous criteria.

*Step 3.2. Temporal effects analysis.* The following are evaluated for each critical service: (a) the time required for the manifestation of maximum impact and (b) the time required to fully restore a service after a possible attack manifestation. Time analysis is used for the classification of critical services within each level of criticality. Temporal analysis is used for prioritizing services within the same criticality level. Specifically, depending on the scores for (a) and (b) each critical element is assigned to a specific category (Step 3.3).

*Step 3.3. Indirect criticality rating.* Any possible critical service is also analyzed based on the indirect effects that can cause during a failure scenario. Indirect effects depend on two factors:

– Dependencies of the service in question with other critical services. Whether and how much other critical elements may depend on this particular service.
– Evaluation of indirect criticality is performed by utilizing one or more horizontal criteria, from Step 3.1.

*Results.* The list of prioritized sub-sectors and services per sub-sector, as well as a table of interdependencies between sub-sectors/services will be provided as input to Step 4, to assess the criticality of (sub) systems per critical service. This step determines a list of possible European critical sectors/subsectors or services. For each horizontal criterion to be applied, criticality levels are described using a quality scale (e.g. Low, Medium, High). For each level, a minimum quantitative impact threshold is set.

**STEP 4: Evaluating Critical (sub) systems per service**

*Short description.* For each critical service, a list of involved owners-managers is compiled, from which (or in collaboration with whom) a second list of the most critical subsystems that support this service is compiled.

*Implementation.* According to the approach proposed by the EPCIP framework [5, 6], certain criteria must be applied at each sub-sector for the characterization of a subsystem as a possible CI inside a service (Step 4.1). This is to check whether a subsystem meets at least one horizontal criticality criterion (Step 4.2).

*Results.* This step provides a list of the most critical subsystems per service. This will be the actual list of national CI, according to the 114/2008/EC Directive. As part of a National CI Protection Program, CI owners-operators in collaboration with a qualified national body must identify the most important assets per critical subsystem and develop Operation Security Plans (OSP) and Contingency Plans (CP) to protect the CI (Annex II - 114/2008/EC Directive).

*Step 4.*1: *Application of Sectoral Criteria*: Sectoral criteria are technical or operational criteria used to identify potential critical subsystems. These criteria do not report, although hint, potential repercussions (e.g. obstruction or shutdown of a subsystem). Instead, they only refer to certain inherent characteristics. In particular, the sectoral criteria may refer to [5, 6]:

- Technical properties. For example, quantifiable characteristics, such as dimensions, capacities, distances, speed, data volume, etc.
- Non-technical properties. For example, identifiable features such as recovery time, recovery costs etc.

To identify a subsystem as potentially critical, it should exceed a predetermined threshold (threshold) concerning the values of some sectoral criteria.

*Step 4.*2: *Application of Horizontal Criteria*: For each subsystem that provides essential services, we assess the severity that its loss or dysfunction would have on society. A subsystem is critical when it meets at least one of the horizontal criticality criteria, concerning the direct (Step 3.1) or indirect criticality (Step 3.2). Also, criticality evaluation takes into account parameters such as the availability of alternatives, the turning-point for "painful" consequences, as well as the time needed for recovery.

**STEP 5: Periodic re-assessment of CI**

*Short description.* All critical and relevant factors concerning the criticality of a CI and relevant services should be reassessed after some time by applying all steps of the methodology at regular intervals.

*Input data.* All results of the previous evaluation of critical components (sectors, sub-sectors, services, systems).

*Implementation.* The reassessment may be general (step 1, taking into account the previous critical services list), or may refer to a particular sector/subsector (step 3) or service (step 4). The reassessment scope is determined by a qualified body in collaboration with stakeholders. The need for reassessment should be determined on a mid-term basis; the period must be fixed in advance, regardless of whether changes in the collected data occur or not.

*Results.* The amended list of critical elements and CI or the update of the previous assessment of critical components (domains, subdomains, services and systems).

### 3.1 Applying Evaluation Criteria on Candidate National CI

After establishing all parameters for evaluating potential CI, the description of the national CI assessment methodology is complete and will now be applied to the Greek Energy and ICT sectors. During the implementation of the horizontal evaluation criteria, the estimated impact always refers to the worst-case scenario.

Therefore, when analyzing potential impact values listed in the tables below, the value attributed to each impact corresponds to the most negative potential effect that is likely to occur.

Also when we applied the criteria, there happened to be some cases where the assessment could not get unique value assignments, thus values were assigned on the 1–2 impact scale. When a qualified national body implements a full version of the above methodology, every service criterion should be assigned only one scale value.

### Energy Sector evaluation

The Energy Sector includes the following sub-sectors: Electricity, Oil and Natural Gas. Tables 5, 6 and 7 summarize the evaluation of each sub-sector and key dependencies recorded, incoming and outgoing, by sub-sector.

**Table 5.** Application of Criteria - Electricity subsector

| Services | Direct assessment (Horizontal Criteria) | | | | | Time criteria | | Indirect |
|---|---|---|---|---|---|---|---|---|
| | Geographic al width | Economic Loss | Human casualties | Environmental Cons. | Consequences to the Public | Time of consequence manifestation | Recovery Time | assessment (due to dependencies) |
| Production of electrical power | Territory | Important % of GNP | Potential Loss in case of accident | Potential in case of accident | Effect on the lives of million citizens | Rapid consequence manifestation Slow recovery | | Affects most CIs |
| | LEVEL 3 | LEVEL 3 | LEVEL 1 | LEVEL 1 | LEVEL 3 | CATEGORY 3 | | LEVEL 3 |
| Transportation/Distribution of electrical power | Territory | Important % of GNP | Potential Loss due to impact on Health Sector | | Effect on the lives of million citizens | Rapid consequence manifestation Slow recovery | | Affects most CIs |
| | LEVEL 3 | LEVEL 3 | LEVEL 1 | | LEVEL 3 | CATEGORY 3 | | LEVEL 3 |
| Electrical power market | Territory | Important % of GNP | | | Effect on the lives of million citizens | Rapid consequence manifestation Slow recovery | | Affects most CIs |
| | LEVEL 3 | LEVEL 3 | | | LEVEL 3 | CATEGORY 2 | | LEVEL 3 |

Based on the application of the evaluation criteria and taking into account the record from providers/-operators per service, our evaluation provided the following:

- In the Electricity sub-sector all services are assessed as high critical, both for direct and indirect dependencies. To an extent, they also depend on one provider/IM (PPC).
- Concerning the temporal analysis of impact, the Production and Distribution services have higher priority than the electricity market service, as far as recovery time is concerned.
- At the subsystems level, all subsystems used to support this sector's services must be tested using corresponding sectoral criteria.

**Table 6.** Application of criteria - oil subsector

| Services | Direct Assessment (Horizontal Criteria) | | | | | Time criteria | | Indirect assessment (due to dependencies) |
| | Geographical width | Economic loss | Human casualties | Environmental Cons. | Consequences to the Public | Time of consequence manifestation | Recovery Time | |
|---|---|---|---|---|---|---|---|---|
| Oil extraction | | | May cause loss of life | Serious consequences | | | | |
| | | | LEVEL 1 | LEVEL 1 or LEVEL 2 | | | | |
| Oil refinement | Territory | Important % of GNP | May cause loss of life | Serious consequences | Effect on the lives of million citizens | Slow consequence manifestation Slow recovery | | Affects most CIs |
| | LEVEL 3 | LEVEL 3 | LEVEL 1 | LEVEL 1 or LEVEL 2 | LEVEL 3 | CATEGORY 2 | | LEVEL 3 |
| Oil transportation | Territory | Important % of GNP | May cause loss of life | Serious consequences | Effect on the lives of million citizens | Slow consequence manifestation Slow recovery | | Affects most CIs |
| | LEVEL 3 | LEVEL 3 | LEVEL 1 | LEVEL 1 or LEVEL 2 | LEVEL 3 | CATEGORY 2 | | LEVEL 3 |
| Oil storage | Territory | Important % of GNP | May cause loss of life | Serious consequences | Effect on the lives of million citizens | Slow consequence manifestation Slow recovery | | Affects most CIs |
| | LEVEL 3 | LEVEL 3 | LEVEL 1 or LEVEL 2 | LEVEL 1 or LEVEL 2 | LEVEL 3 | CATEGORY 2 | | LEVEL 3 |

**Table 7.** Application of criteria - natural gas subsector

| Services | Direct Assessment (Horizontal Criteria) | | | | | Time Criteria | | Indirect Assessment (due to dependencies) |
| | Geographical width | Economic Loss | Human Casualties | Environmental Cons. | Consequences to the Public | Time of consequence manifestation | Recovery Time | |
|---|---|---|---|---|---|---|---|---|
| Transportation & distribution of natural gas | Territory | Important % of GNP | Potential loss in case of accident | Low consequences | Effect on the lives of million citizens | Rapid consequence manifestation Slow recovery | | Affects > 2 CIs (Industry, Electricity Production) |
| | LEVEL 3 | LEVEL 3 or LEVEL 2 | LEVEL 1 or LEVEL 2 | LEVEL 1 or LEVEL 0 | LEVEL 3 | CATEGORY 3 | | LEVEL 3 |
| Natural Gas storage | Territory | Important % of GNP | Potential loss due to impact on health sector | Low consequences | Effect on the lives of million citizens | Rapid consequence manifestation Slow recovery | | Affects > 2 CIs (Industry, Electricity Production) |
| | LEVEL 3 | LEVEL 3/LEVEL 2 | LEVEL 1/LEVEL 2 | LEVEL 1/LEVEL 0 | LEVEL 3 | CATEGORY 2 | | LEVEL 3 |

## ICT Sector evaluation

The ICT sector includes the Telecommunications and Information Technologies sub-sectors. Table 8 presents the evaluation of these subsectors.

Based on the application of the evaluation criteria and taking into account the record from providers/operators per service, our evaluation provided the following:

- The Communications sub-sector has increased impact in Greece. All services showed that they are of high criticality, both in direct and in indirect evaluations of

**Table 8.** Application of Criteria - Telecommunications subsector

| Services | Direct Assessment (Horizontal Criteria) | | | | | Time Criteria | | Indirect Assessment (due to dependencies) |
|---|---|---|---|---|---|---|---|---|
| | Geographical width | Economic Loss | Human Casualties | Environmental Cons. | Consequences to the Public | Time of consequence manifestation | Recovery Time | |
| Voice/Data communication services | Territory | Important % of GNP | Potential Loss due to impact on Health Sector | – | Effect on the lives of million citizens | Rapid consequence manifestation Rapid recovery | | Affects most CIs |
| | LEVEL 3 | LEVEL 3 or LEVEL 2 | LEVEL 1 | | LEVEL 3 | CATEGORY 2 | | LEVEL 3 |
| Internet Provision | Territory | Important % of GNP | Potential Loss due to impact on Health Sector | – | Effect on the lives of million citizens | Rapid consequence manifestation Rapid recovery | | Affects most CIs |
| | LEVEL 3 | LEVEL 3 or LEVEL 2 | LEVEL 1 | | LEVEL 3 | CATEGORY 2 | | LEVEL 3 |

dependencies. The Communications sub-sector services depend to a large extent, from a single provider (OTE).

- Concerning the temporal analysis of impact, it was shown that both the voice/data communication services and the provision of Internet services present fast impact effects but rapid recovery times, thus fall within the same priority level.

**Acknowledgments.** This work was performed within the *OLIKY* project framework. OLIKY was coordinated by the INFOSEC Laboratory (Athens University of Economics & Business) and funded by *diaNEOsis*, a non-government and non-profit research and analysis organization, located in Greece. The opinions expressed herein are those of the authors.

# References

1. EU Commission: Communication from the Commission on a European Programme for Critical Infrastructure Protection COM (2006) 786 final (2006)
2. EU Commission: European Commission, staff working document on the review of the European Programme for Critical Infrastructure Protection (EPCIP), Brussels (2012)
3. EU Commission: European Commission, staff working document on a new approach to the European Programme for Critical Infrastructure Protection making European Critical Infrastructures more secure), Brussels, Belgium (2013)
4. EU Commission 149: European Commission. Protecting Europe from large scale cyber-attacks and disruptions: enhancing preparedness, security and resilience (2009)
5. EU Council: Council of the European Union, Non-Binding Guidelines for the application of the Directive on the identification and designation of European Critical Infrastructure and the assessment of the need to improve their protection, Brussels [14808/08] (2008b)
6. EU Council: Proposal for a COUNCIL DECISION on a Critical Infrastructure Warning Information Network (CIWIN). COM (2008) 676 final (2008c)
7. ENISA, Mattioli, R., Levy-Bencheton, C.: Methodologies for the identification of Critical Information Infrastructure assets and services. ENISA Report, December 2014 (2014)

8. Faily, S., Stergiopoulos, G., Katos, V., Gritzalis, D.: "Water, Water, Every Where": nuances for a water industry critical infrastructure specification exemplar. In: Rome, E., Theocharidou, M., Wolthusen, S. (eds.) CRITIS 2015. LNCS, vol. 9578, pp. 243–246. Springer, Cham (2016). doi:10.1007/978-3-319-33331-1_20

9. FC: Federal council's basic strategy for critical infrastructure protection, basis for the national critical infrastructure protection strategy. In: Confédération Swisse, 18 May 2009 (2009)

10. French Strategy: French national digital security strategy. French Republic (2015)

11. FRG: National Strategy for Critical Infrastructure Protection (CIP Strategy). Federal Ministry of the Interior, Federal Republic of Germany. Berlin, June 17 2009

12. Klaver, M., Luiijf, H., Nieuwenhuijsen, A.: RECIPE: Good practices manual for CIP policies, for policy makers in Europe (2011)

13. Kotzanikolaou, P., Theocharidou, M., Gritzalis, D.: Accessing n-order dependencies between critical infrastructures. Int. J. Crit. Infrastruct. Prot. 9(1–2), 93–110 (2013)

14. Kotzanikolaou, P., Theoharidou, M., Gritzalis, D.: Cascading effects of common-cause failures in critical infrastructures. In: Butts, J., Shenoi, S. (eds.) ICCIP 2013. IAICT, vol. 417, pp. 171–182. Springer, Heidelberg (2013). doi:10.1007/978-3-642-45330-4_12

15. Kotzanikolaou, P., Theoharidou, M., Gritzalis, D.: Interdependencies between critical infrastructures: analyzing the risk of cascading effects. In: Bologna, S., Hämmerli, B., Gritzalis, D., Wolthusen, S. (eds.) CRITIS 2011. LNCS, vol. 6983, pp. 104–115. Springer, Heidelberg (2013). doi:10.1007/978-3-642-41476-3_9

16. Lebau-Marianna, D., Roger, E.: France – three decrees reinforced the safety obligations of Operators of Vital Importance, 8 July 2015

17. Livre Blanc: Défense et sécurité nationale, République Francaise (2013)

18. Luiijf, E., Burger, H., Klaver, M.: Critical infrastructure protection in the Netherlands: a quick-scan. In: EICAR Conference Best Paper Proceedings (Vol. 19). Denmark (2003)

19. MSB: A first step towards a national risk assessment. Swedish Civil Contingencies Agency-MSB, Sweden (2011). 2011

20. MSB: Action Plan for the Protection of Vital Societal Functions & Critical Infrastructure. Swedish Civil Contingencies Agency, Risk & Vulnerability Reduction Department (2014)

21. Renda, A., Hammerli, B. (2010). Protecting critical infrastructure in the EU. CEPS Task Force Report

22. Salonikias, S., Mavridis, I., Gritzalis, D.: Access control issues in utilizing fog computing for transport infrastructure. In: Rome, E., Theocharidou, M., Wolthusen, S. (eds.) CRITIS 2015. LNCS, vol. 9578, pp. 15–26. Springer, Cham (2016). doi:10.1007/978-3-319-33331-1_2

23. Stergiopoulos, G., Kotzanikolaou, P., Theocharidou, M., Gritzalis, D.: Risk mitigation strategies for critical infrastructures based on graph centrality analysis. Int. J. Crit. Infrastruct. Prot. 10, 34–44 (2015)

24. Stergiopoulos, G., Kotzanikolaou, P., Theocharidou, M., Lykou, G., Gritzalis, D.: Time-base critical infrastructure dependency analysis for large-scale and cross-sectoral failures. Int. J. Crit. Infrastruct. Prot. 12, 46–60 (2016)

25. Theocharidou, M., Kandias, M., Gritzalis, D.: Securing transportation-critical infrastructures: trends and perspectives. In: Georgiadis, C.K., Jahankhani, H., Pimenidis, E., Bashroush, R., Al-Nemrat, A. (eds.) Global Security, Safety and Sustainability & e-Democracy. LNICST, vol. 99, pp. 171–178. Springer, Berlin, Heidelberg (2012). doi:10.1007/978-3-642-33448-1_24

26. UK: Strategic Framework and Policy Statement on Improving the Resilience of Critical Infrastructure to Disruption from Natural Hazards (2010)

# Full Papers

# A Security Policy Infrastructure
# for Tactical Service Oriented Architectures

Vasileios Gkioulos[1(✉)] and Stephen D. Wolthusen[1,2]

[1] Norwegian Information Security Laboratory,
Norwegian University of Science and Technology, Gjøvik, Norway
{vasileios.gkioulos,stephen.wolthusen}@ntnu.no
[2] School of Mathematics and Information Security, Royal Holloway,
University of London, Egham, UK

**Abstract.** Tactical networks are affected by multiple constraints related
to the limited node characteristics and the availability of resources. These
constraints within the highly dynamic tactical environment, impose significant limitations to the functionalities and efficiency of current generic
security policy frameworks.

Earlier studies have provided a risk analysis of tactical service oriented
architectures (SOA), and a set of fine-grained protection goals in corre-
spondence to the aforementioned constraints. Furthermore, web ontology
language has been identified as a suitable mediator towards the requirements and opportunities imposed by tactical SOA. Thus, in this article
we present a security policy framework dedicated to tactical networks,
as it has been developed within the project TACTICS.

**Keywords:** Ad-Hoc · Policy · Security · Service oriented architectures ·
Tactical networks

## 1 Introduction

Tactical networks are of Ad-Hoc nature, subjected to a variety of constraints
related both to the limited operational characteristics of the deployed nodes and
the scarcity of network resources. Such constraints impede the attainment of
requisite protection goals, by rendering current generic solutions unsuitable, due
to limited adaptability over the network dynamics. For that purpose, within the
project TACTICS (TACTICal Service oriented architecture), suitable security
solutions have been developed, tailored to the characteristics of tactical service
oriented architectures. Within this scope our study aims to identify and support
fine-grained protection goals over the initial over provisioned operational stages,
but mainly through the anticipated degraded and disrupted mission execution
phases.

Earlier studies [1,2] presented a detailed risk analysis of tactical SOA, investigating the impact of the aforementioned constraints across the three stages
of tactical operations (Preparation-Execution-Debrief). Furthermore, suitable

© Springer International Publishing AG 2017
N. Cuppens-Boulahia et al. (Eds.): CyberICPS 2016, LNCS 10166, pp. 37–51, 2017.
DOI: 10.1007/978-3-319-61437-3_3

security requirements and protection goals have been identified, referring to the security of communication procedures, transitive information, data at rest and service choreography related processes. Finally, the feasible benefits of exploiting the unique characteristics of service oriented architectures have been identified, aiming to utilise them for the enhancement of the implemented security mechanisms.

The results of these studies have been consequently utilised for the extraction of functional requirements in respect to the developed security policy mechanisms [3–5]. These requirements include constraints related to scalability, real time dynamic adaptability, cross layer implementation and distributed deployment. A parallel evaluation between the identified functional policy requirements and the constraints imposed by the nature of tactical SOA, was undertaken for the examination of suitable security policy frameworks. This examination included commonly used mechanisms, such as WS - Security, SAML [6], XACML [7] and Ponder [8], as well as recent semantic (REI [9], KAOS [10], ROWLBAC [11], Kolter et al. [12], Trivellato et al. [13]) and trust management frameworks (cassandra [14], Tulip [15], RT [16], Peer-Trust [17]). This analysis promoted the use of web ontology language (OWL) as the most suitable solution in respect to the requirements of tactical SOA. Thus, the same study presented a tactical policy framework and our initial results regarding its conceptualisation.

In this paper we present a detailed analysis of this security policy framework dedicated to tactical SOA, as it has been designed within TACTICS. Section 2 introduces the developed tactical service infrastructure, focusing on the security related services, their interactions and functionalities. Section 3 presents the core policy model in accordance to the decision process, along with the required steps for the policy formalization. Finally, Sect. 4 includes a simplified example of the prototype implementation developed for validation and demonstration purposes.

## 2   Tactical Service Infrastructure-TSI

Four distinct instances of tactical nodes have been assumed within TACTICS, each of whom supports the delivery of a defined associated functionality set, through standard interfaces. The studied tactical node types are:

- TSI Node-Dismounted: Carried by individual soldiers.
- TSI Node-Mobile: Integrated in single vehicles.
- TSI Node-HQ: Integrated in semi-permanent headquarters.
- TSI Node-Custom: Unmanned operational node.

The internal TSI components along with a subset of the defined core functionalities are presented at Fig. 1, while the security related services are highlighted (Yellow). The middle-ware has been divided into two vertical stacks, as it was presented in detail by Thorsten et al. [18] namely:

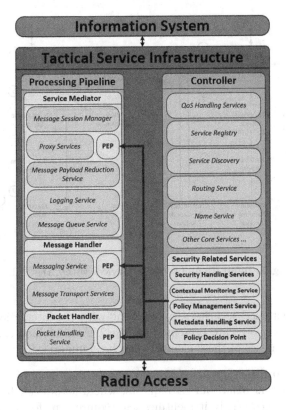

**Fig. 1.** Defined internal components of TSI nodes. (Color figure online)

1. **Processing Pipeline:** It comprise of the following sub-components:
   - *Service Mediator:* Supports functionalities related to session management, message exchange and message adaptation. The defined functionalities include but are not limited to locate remote services, create proxy services, support various message exchange patterns and adjust message priority.
   - *Message Handler:* Supports functionalities related to message forwarding and message transport. The defined functionalities include but are not limited to message format translation, next hop identification, message monitoring and message storage management.
   - *Packet Handler:* Supports functionalities related to packet forwarding and packet scheduling. The defined functionalities include but are not limited to reliability handling, packet queue handling and packet release to radio.
2. **Controller:** It includes core services responsible for the supervision of the aforementioned services, deployed across the processing pipeline layers. The defined functionalities include but are not limited to trigger resource reservation, update service endpoints, select routing protocol and enforce encryption mechanisms.

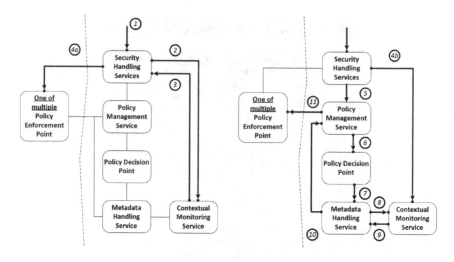

**Fig. 2.** Interaction of security services within the TSI.

The aforementioned security services along with the interactions supported by the defined interfaces are presented at Fig. 2. As described earlier in detail [19], the functionalities of these elements can be summarised as:

- **Security Handling Service-(SH):** A service that monitors network parameters and actors behaviour or requests, where actors can be users, nodes and services. Accordingly it identifies the requirement for a specific action, initiating a corresponding action request. Additionally, SH stores precomputed policy decisions, either from the mission preparation stage or by earlier requests during mission execution, for optimization of resource utilization.
- **Policy Management Service-(PM):** A service that is responsible for the successful resolution of the action request in accordance to the current network parameters and its subsequent transfer for enforcement.
- **Policy Decision Point-(PDP):** It contains the policy rules mapped to the available action requests, in the form of prioritised description logic queries.
- **Metadata Handling Service-(MH):** An ontological knowledge-base that incorporates static and dynamic attributes required for reasoning over the aforementioned policy rules. Reasoning occurs at the MH in accordance to a static copy of the ontological structure at the time of the action request in order to maintain policy consistency.
- **Contextual Monitoring Service-(CM):** A service that monitors timely values of the dynamic attributes utilised across the policy rules, while it computes statistical and aggregated values populating MH upon request.
- **Policy Enforcement Point-(PEP):** A service responsible for the enforcement of the generated or precomputed policy decisions, by use of the locally implemented mechanisms.

While in respect to the functionalities of the implemented interfaces:

– **1:** SH receives a trigger for the initiation of an action request. The trigger can be either external (e.g. Access request by a user, service invocation request by a service, message prioritization request by Quality of Service (Qos) mechanisms) or internal by monitoring the values of the dynamic attributes stored at CM (e.g. node trust levels, node location updates, service choreography statistics).
– **2:** SH requests from CM the current values of the attributes related to the given action request. These values are compared with a predefined range for which the precomputed policy decisions are valid.
– **3:** CM replies with the timely values of the requested dynamic attributes.
– **4a:** If the received attribute values correspond to the predefined ranges, the precomputed policy decision is transferred to the corresponding PEP for enforcement. In this scenario the procedure is successfully terminated at this stage.
– **4b:** If the received attribute values are outside the predefined ranges, SH sends a request to CM for a static copy of the monitored parameters with a unique identifier.
– **5:** SH sends an action solution request to the PM including the unique identifier.
– **6:** PM sends the same bundle (Action Solution Request, Unique Identifier) to the PDP, which retrieves the stored set of prioritised rules corresponding to the given action request.
– **7:** PDP populates the bundle with the first priority rule (Action Solution Request, Unique Identifier, 1st Priority Rule) and transfers it to the MH.
– **8:** MH requests the values of the monitored parameters corresponding to the received Unique Identifier.
– **9:** MH receives the aforementioned values and populates a locally stored copy of the ontological knowledge-base. At this stage, reasoning occurs using this copy and the received 1st Priority Rule.
– **10:** The identified instances are transferred to PM. (Note: If no instances have been identified, steps 6 to 10 are repeated using the complementary prioritised rules)
– **11:** The policy decision is transferred to the PEP for enforcement.

## 3   Formal Policy Modelling

### 3.1   Core Policy Model

The formal policy model has been constructed by mapping the aforementioned architectural elements to the required functionalities, as presented at Fig. 3. The decision process within the formal policy model is:

$$Individual\_Domain \cap Individual\_Capability = \{Individual\_Action(k),$$
$$Individual\_Action(k+1), ..., Individual\_Action(k+i)\} \quad (1)$$

where:

$$Individual\_Action(k) \widehat{=} \{Individual\_Rule[k(z)], Individual\_Rule[k(z+1)], ..., \\ Individual\_Rule[k(z+j)]\} \quad (2)$$

And:

$$Observable\_Objects \xrightarrow{Individual\_Rulek(z)} Governing\_Mechanisms_{Individual\_Action(k)} \quad (3)$$

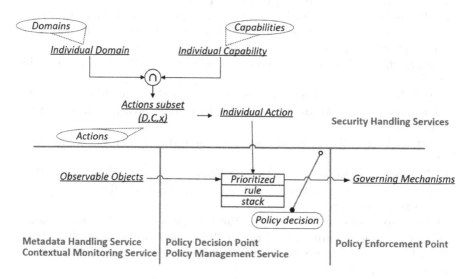

**Fig. 3.** Visualisation of the decision process within the formal policy model.

While the elements constituting the formal policy model have been defined as:

- **Domains:** The tactical policy domains have been identified in accordance to the protection requirements as Planning, Protection, Detection, Diligence and Response. These generic core domains can be extended or refined in order to support fine-grained definition of policy governance.
  - **Individual Domain:** A singular Domain corresponding to the evaluated action.
- **Capabilities:** TACTICS defined a distinct set of capabilities as part of the developed Tactical Reference Architecture (TRA), in accordance to contemporary operational requirements and the existing NATO Capability View (NAF-NCV-2/7 [20]). The extended list of defined capabilities includes Effects Management, Fire Support, Combat Service Support and Shared Situational Awareness.

– **Individual Capability:** A singular Capability corresponding to the evaluated action.
– **Actions:** Actions are defined as the intersection of Domains and Capabilities, in the sense of enforcing the Domain requirements upon the operational Capabilities. Thus, defining fine grained policy sub-trees such as Planning/Effect Management, Protection/Shared Situational Awareness or Response/Intrusion Detection.
– **Actions subset:** A subset of available,suitable and prioritised responses in respect to the defined Actions, by the activation and tailored management of the available Governing Mechanisms. In that sense the Action "Protection/Message Transmission", may correspond to an Action subset that includes various cryptographic and credential management services
– **Individual Action:** A singular policy response across the examined Action subset.

*Note: The definition of these elements allow the Security Handling Services to identify and initiate fine-grained policy decisions, as mapped in a prioritised order to the monitored Observable Objects and actor behaviour or requests.*

– **Observable Objects:** Monitored network parameters of static and dynamic nature, as predefined during the mission preparation stage. Observable Objects refer to Service, Information, Network, Radio, Node and Subject attributes, formulating a complete description of the tactical SOA ecosystem upon which policy reasoning is achieved.

*Note: The Metadata Handling Service maintains a static local knowledge according to the values of Observable Objects in an ontological knowledge base, while the Contextual Monitoring Service is responsible for the monitoring of dynamic Observable Objects and the calculation of their timely, statistical and aggregated values.*

– **Prioritized rule stack:** A set of predefined and prioritized rules dedicated to the governance of each Individual Action. Every rule is constructed as a description logic query for instance identification, with increased granularity as a function of Observable Objects.

*Note: The definition of multiple rules for the governance of each Individual Action allows the on-line adaptation of policy decisions to the dynamic network conditions, in contrast to singular implementations. The communication between the Policy Decision Point and Policy Management Service facilitates the selection of the most suitable governing rule at the decision time, according to predefined prioritizations*

– **Governing Mechanisms:** Services deployed within the Policy Decision Point capable of enforcing the policy decision in respect to an examined Individual Action.

*Note: The deployed Governing Mechanisms can be generic or mission specific, related to a variety of security requirements such as authentication, authorisation, cryptography, session management, access control, integrity control, error handling/logging, validation and public key infrastructure.*

## 3.2  Policy Formalization

The formalisation of the core policy model elements within the security TSI services, is based on suitable description logic fragments and executed in six consecutive steps. These steps are in direct mapping to the decision process, as presented in Eqs. 1, 2 and 3. Various detailed resources exist in respect to knowledge representation with description logic [21]. Thus, the purpose of this subsection is not to provide an exhaustive reference to this topic, but an insight to the elements crucial for the formalization of the developed security policy model:

- **Equation 1**
  – *Step 1-Definition of Domains:*
  Individual Domains are initially formalised as empty disjoint ontology classes, using terminological box concept definitions. These classes are consequently populated with the defined Actions, formalising extensional knowledge in the form of simple membership assertions, as:

$$hasDomain(AccessDenial, Response) \tag{4}$$

A closed world assumption must be enforced in order to accommodate the functionality of the Security Handling Services in respect to Action identification. This is achieved in ontology editors by the definition of restricted equivalences for each domain class using a functional data property (e.g. has-Domain). As an example in OWL functional syntax, this is defined as:

*Declaration(Class(:Domains))*
*Declaration(Class(:Response))*
*SubClassOf(:Response :Domains)*
*EquivalentClasses(:Response DataHasValue(:hasDomain "Response"))*
*Declaration(DataProperty(:hasDomain))*
*FunctionalDataProperty(:hasDomain)*
*DataPropertyRange(:hasDomain DataOneOf("Defined Domains"))*
*Declaration(NamedIndividual(:AccessDenial))*
*DataPropertyAssertion(:hasDomain :AccessDenial "Response" xsd:string)*

  – *Step 2-Definition of Capabilities:*
  Capabilities are formalised and populated similarly to Domains, as:
  *Declaration(Class(:Capabilities))*
  *Declaration(Class(:MessageAuthenticityAssurance))*
  *SubClassOf(:MessageAuthenticityAssurance :Capabilities)*
  *EquivalentClasses(:MessageAuthenticityAssurance*
  *DataHasValue(:hasCapability "MessageAuthenticityAssurance"))*
  *Declaration(DataProperty(:hasCapability))*
  *FunctionalDataProperty(:hasCapability)*
  *DataPropertyRange(:hasCapability DataOneOf("Defined Capabilities"))*
  *Declaration(NamedIndividual(:DigitalSignatureValidation))*

*DataPropertyAssertion(:hasCapability :DigitalSignatureValidation*
*"MessageAuthenticityAssurance" xsd:string)*

*– Step 3-Definition of Actions and Grouping into Actions subsets:*
Actions are formalised as individuals with the use of unary predicates and
categorised into Action subsets with the use of existential quantifications
and value restrictions. This is achieved in ontology editors with the definition of data properties of suitable granularity. As mentioned earlier, the
Security Handling Service initiates an Action based policy request in accordance to external or internal triggers. An external trigger is directed to
a singular Action (e.g. Domain:Protection/Capability:ServiceAccessControl/
Action:AccessMessagingService), but an internal trigger is based on the
dynamic values of predefined Observable Objects leading to the identification
and evaluation of multiple actions defined as an Action subset. Thus the Actions
forming each Action subset must be prioritised in order to accommodate this
functionality, allowing the identification and enforcement of the most suitable
policy decision in accordance to the existing resources. Description logic allows
the fine-grained definition of Actions. In the previous simplified example, the
Action definition is represented in OWL functional syntax as:

*Declaration(DataProperty(:hasActionSetID))*
*Declaration(DataProperty(:hasActionSetPriority))*
*Declaration(DataProperty(:hasCapability))*
*Declaration(DataProperty(:hasDomain))*
*Declaration(DataProperty(:hasGoverningMechanism))*
*Declaration(DataProperty(:hasRuleSetID))*
*Declaration(NamedIndividual(:AccessMessagingService))*
*FunctionalDataProperty(:hasActionSetID)*
*DataPropertyRange(:hasActionSetID xsd:integer)*
*FunctionalDataProperty(:hasActionSetPriority)*
*DataPropertyRange(:hasActionSetPriority xsd:integer)*
*FunctionalDataProperty(:hasCapability)*
*DataPropertyRange(:hasCapability DataOneOf("Defined Capabilities"))*
*FunctionalDataProperty(:hasDomain)*
*DataPropertyRange(:hasDomain DataOneOf("Defined Domains"))*
*DataPropertyRange(:hasGoverningMechanism xsd:string)*
*FunctionalDataProperty(:hasRuleSetID)*
*DataPropertyRange(:hasRuleSetID xsd:integer)*
*DataPropertyAssertion(:hasActionSetID :AccessMessagingService*
*"9632654" xsd:integer)*
*DataPropertyAssertion(:hasActionSetPriority :AccessMessagingService*
*"1" xsd:integer)*
*DataPropertyAssertion(:hasCapability :AccessMessagingService*
*"ServiceAccessControl" xsd:string)*
*DataPropertyAssertion(:hasDomain :AccessMessagingService*
*"Protection" xsd:string)*

*DataPropertyAssertion(:hasGoverningMechanism :AccessMessagingService*
*"AuthServ23" xsd:string)*
*DataPropertyAssertion(:hasRuleSetID :AccessMessagingService*
*"86514665" xsd:integer)*

It must be noted that in terms of ease of implementation and deployment, the same procedure can be used for the definition of Action clusters according to invocation and statistical patterns. Utilising constrained class equivalences and exceptions, Actions of separate Action subsets can be efficiently grouped and mapped into common policy rules, significantly minimising resource consumption under heavily constrained scenarios.

– **Equation** 2
 *– Step 4-Definition of Prioritised rule stack per Action:*
 The notable expressive power of description logic fragments originates from the extended set of available constructors, including but not limited to elements of first order logic (e.g. intersection, union, complement, universal/ existential restriction) and role oriented (e.g. role union/ chains/ transitivity/ hierarchy). The full extend of available constructors can be exploited at this step for the definition of detailed rules of increased granularity, incorporating both unary and binary predicates in accordance to the security requirements. Thus, a prioritized rule stack of increasing complexity is defined per Action, facilitating the adaptation of the security policy to dynamic network conditions. The least-priority/least-complexity rule for each Action is defined as a default escape policy expression (i.e. deny-override, permit-override, deny-by-default, permit-by-default) depending on the type of the Action, for use in highly congested tactical environments and node isolation scenarios. Concurrently, the rules of highest priority can designedly incorporate sets of unary and binary predicates, referring to discrete adaptations of the security policy to the real time network conditions for the given Action.

– **Equation** 3
 *– Step 5-Extraction of Observable Objects and knowledge base construction:*
 Observable Objects correspond to the aforementioned unary and binary predicates referring to service, information, network, radio, node and subject attributes as incorporated within the policy rules. Observable Objects can be defined in ontology editors as object and data properties, enforcing suitable schema constructs (e.g. subPropertyOf, range), relations to other properties (e.g. inverseOf), logical characteristics (e.g. transitive, symmetric) and global cardinality restrictions (e.g. InverseFunctionalProperty, FunctionalProperty). Depending on the granularity requirements of the defined policy rules aggregated and statistical Observable Objects can also be constructed and incorporated, allowing their utilisation across rules of distinct priority levels.
 *– Step 6-Mapping of Individual Actions to Governing Mechanisms:*
 This step is initiated during Step-3 by the definition of suitable DataPropertyAssertions, and finalised by a constrained mapping between actions and suitable Governing Mechanisms for their enforcement. This is achieved by the definition of simple membership assertions, similar to those presented in previous steps.

# 4 Prototype Implementation

TACTICS has defined sixty requirements with "MUST" priority, forty with "SHOULD" and seven with "COULD", thirty-four of which are security dedicated as briefly discussed earlier [1,2]. An overall prototype implementation has been realised according to Sects. 2 and 3, in order to validate the satisfaction of these requirements under the distinct tactical constraints. This implementation was targeted to four common tactical operation types (1-Reconnaissance Surveillance and Target Acquisition, 2-MEDical EVACuation, 3-Convoy mission, 4-Intervention Patrol), separated into a multitude of corresponding episodes (e.g. Sensor data acquisition, Blue force tracking, Mobility management, Improvised Explosive Device detection and report, Ordering and Tasking). Here we present the security policy formalization, in respect to the interface functionalities as presented at Sects. 2 and 3, for one of the investigated episodes.

## 4.1 Transitive Service Invocation

The presented example is part of the transitive service invocation scenarios of the convoy mission use case. Nodes N1 and N2 are mounted on vehicles that belong to a tactical convoy, with N1 being the command vehicle and N3 a handheld device (TSI Node Dismounted) allocated to a member of N2 personnel. The scenes of the episode are:

1. N1 requires an image from the Area of Operation(AoO) of N2
2. N1 Identifies available services*
3. N1 Identifies local service provider*
4. N1 Transmits corresponding request to N2
5. N2 Transmits corresponding request to N3
6. N3 Evaluates service access request*
7. N3 Invokes service
8. N3 Identifies image compression requirement*
9. N3 Identifies local service provider*
10. N3 Transmits uncompressed image to N2
11. N2 Evaluates service access request * (According to image attributes and N3 credentials)
12. N2 Invokes service
13. N2 Transmits compressed image to N1

The overall execution of a transitive service invocation corresponds to a variety of Actions including interactions between the Information System, TSI, and Radio Access, with load both on the northbound/southbound interfaces and core service invocations within and across the involved tactical nodes. For clarity these functionalities have been distributed across multiple use cases, while those corresponding to this scenario are marked as "*". Although multiple security policy decisions are involved within a transitive service invocation, this scenario is one of those dedicated to investigating specific aspects of the service choreography

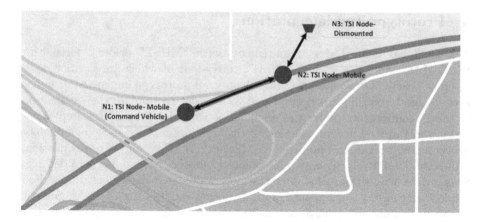

**Fig. 4.** Visualisation of transitive service invocation scenario.

functionalities. Thus, actions related to message transmission and queuing, bandwidth allocation or service substitution refer to the invocation of a variety of TSI core services [18], which are not within the scope of this scenario (Fig. 4).

The policy formalisation in OWL functional syntax for the presented steps 1–6, can be extracted for this episode as:

– *Step 1-Definition of Domain:*
  Only the Protection Domain is required within the given scenario, defined as presented as Sect. 3.2.
– *Step 2-Definition of Capabilities:*
  The given scenario refers to the Service_Choreography and Situational_Awareness capabilities, defined as presented as Sect. 3.2.
– *Step 3-Definition of Actions and Grouping into Actions subsets:*
  The presented functionalities correspond to four of the Actions within the Action subsets defined by the Protection/Service_Choreography and Protection/Situational_Awareness intersections, namely:
  1. Service_ServiceAvailabilityIdentification
  2. Node_LocalServiceProviderIdentification
  3. Service_ServiceAccessRequestVerification
  4. Information_ImageAttributeIdentification
  which are defined as presented as Sect. 3.2.
– *Step 4-Definition of Prioritised rule stack per action:*
  As described earlier, making use of the extended expressive power of description logic allows the construction of complex security policy rules, validating unary and binary predicates as needed by the specific Action. Using as a simplified example the Node_LocalServiceProviderIdentification Action the Prioritised rule stack in Manchester syntax can have the form:
  1. 1st priority rule:
     Node_SupportsService value "TacticsImaging"
     Node_hasUser some AllSubjects

(User_hasTrustLevel value "High") and
((Node_hasTrustLevel value "High") or (Node_hasTrustLevel value "Medium"))
Node_hasAoO value "AoO12341"
(User_hasRank value "COL") or (User_hasRank value "CPT")
Node_hasMissionType value "Convoy"
(Node_hasOperationalGroup value "G2") and (Node_hasType value "TSI_ND")
Node_hasSupportRadioITUDesignation value "UHF"
Node_hasSupportProtocol value "TLS/SSH"

2. 2nd priority rule:
Node_SupportsService value "TacticsImaging"
Node_hasUser some AllSubjects
(User_hasTrustLevel value "High") and
((Node_hasTrustLevel value "High") or (Node_hasTrustLevel value "Medium"))
Node_hasAoO value "AoO12341"
Node_hasOperationalGroup value "G2"
Node_hasSupportRadioITUDesignation value "UHF"
Node_hasSupportProtocol value "TLS/SSH"

3. 3rd priority rule:
Node_SupportsService value "TacticsImaging"
Node_hasUser some AllSubjects
(User_hasTrustLevel value "High") and ((Node_hasTrustLevel value "High") or (Node_hasTrustLevel value "Medium"))
Node_hasAoO value "AoO12341"
Node_hasSupportProtocol value "TLS/SSH"

4. 4th priority rule:
Node_SupportsService value "TacticsImaging"

- *Step 5-Extraction of Observable Objects and knowledge base construction:*
Using the previous rule set as an example the Observable Objects can be extracted as:
1. Data properties (Unary predicates)
User_hasTrustLevel, Node_hasTrustLevel, Node_hasAoO, User_hasRank, Node_hasMissionType, Node_hasOperationalGroup, Node_hasType, Node_hasSupportProtocol
2. Object properties (Binary predicates)
Node_SupportsService, Node_hasUser, Node_hasSupportRadioITUDesignation
The overall extracted Observable Objects incorporated within the security policy knowledge-base are defined as presented as Sect. 3.2 and described earlier [1].

- *Step 6-Mapping of individual Actions to Governing Mechanisms:*
This step depends on the locally implemented services across the nodes deployed for a given tactical operation. Thus, as an example in the given scenario, the Service_ServiceAvailabilityIdentification Action would have as

first priority Governing Mechanism the distributed service registry, while the security policy knowledge-base could also serve as a secondary Governing Mechanism for redundancy purposes.

## 5   Conclusions

In this article we have presented a security policy framework dedicated to tactical SOA, aiming to satisfy the established protection requirements under the constraints of tactical environments. The developed architecture has been presented, focusing on the functionalities of core services and an insight of the defined interfaces. Furthermore, the formal policy model was presented along with the required policy formalisation steps. The prototype implementation has provided a validation of the requirement for an easily deployed, lightweight, cross-layer and dynamically adaptable security infrastructure. Thus, our future plans include the further evaluation with the use of the developed use cases and the preparation of the field-demonstration along with the overall TACTICS architecture.

**Acknowledgments.** The results described in this work were obtained as part of the European Defence Agency project TACTICS (Tactical Service Oriented Architecture). The TACTICS project is jointly undertaken by Patria (FI), Thales Communications & Security (FR), Fraunhofer-Institut für Kommunikation, Informationsverarbeitung und Ergonomie FKIE (DE), Thales Deutschland (DE), Leonardo (IT), Thales Italia (IT), Norwegian University of Science and Technology (NO), ITTI (PL), Military Communication Institute (PL), and their partners, supported by the respective national Ministries of Defence under EDA Contract No. B 0980.

## References

1. Gkioulos, V., Wolthusen, S.D.: Securing tactical service oriented architectures. In: 2nd International Conference on Security of Smart Cities, Industrial Control System and Communications (SSIC) (2016)
2. Aloisio, A., Autili, M., D'Angelo, A., Viidanoja, A., Leguay, J., Ginzler, T., Lampe, T., Spagnolo, L., Wolthusen, S.D., Flizikowski, A., Sliwa, J.: TACTICS: tactical service oriented architecture. CoRR, vol. abs/1504.07578 (2015)
3. Gkioulos, V., Wolthusen, S.D.: Enabling dynamic security policy evaluation for service-oriented architectures in tactical networks. In: Norwegian Information Security Conference 2015 (NISK-2015) (2015)
4. Gkioulos, V., Wolthusen, S.D.: Constraint analysis for security policy partitioning over tactical service oriented architectures. In: Advances in Networking Systems Architectures, Security, and Applications - of Springer's Advances in Intelligent Systems and Computing (2015)
5. Gkioulos, V., Wolthusen, S.D.: Reconciliation of ontologically defined security policies for tactical service oriented architectures. In: International Conference on Future Network Systems and Security-FNSS (2016)
6. OASIS: OASIS Security Services (SAML) TC

7. Ramli, C.D.P.K., Nielson, H.R., Nielson, F.: The logic of XACML. Sci. Comput. Program. **83**, 80–105 (2014)
8. Damianou, N., Dulay, N., Lupu, E., Sloman, M.: The ponder policy specification language. In: Sloman, M., Lupu, E.C., Lobo, J. (eds.) POLICY 2001. LNCS, vol. 1995, pp. 18–38. Springer, Heidelberg (2001). doi:10.1007/3-540-44569-2_2
9. Kagal, L., Finin, T., Paolucci, M., Srinivasan, N., Sycara, K., Denker, G.: Authorization and privacy for semantic web services. IEEE Intell. Syst. **19**, 50–56 (2004)
10. Uszok, A., Bradshaw, J.M., Johnson, M., Jeffers, R., Tate, A., Dalton, J., Aitken, S.: KAoS policy management for semantic web services. IEEE Intell. Syst. **19**, 32–41 (2004)
11. Finin, T., Joshi, A., Kagal, L., Niu, J., Sandhu, R., Winsborough, W.H., Thuraisingham, B.: ROWLBAC - representing role based access control in OWL. In: Proceedings of the 13th Symposium on Access control Models and Technologie, estes Park, Colorado, USA. ACM Press, June 2008
12. Kolter, J., Schillinger, R., Pernul, G.: Building a distributed semantic-aware security architecture. In: Venter, H., Eloff, M., Labuschagne, L., Eloff, J., Solms, R. (eds.) SEC 2007. IIFIP, vol. 232, pp. 397–408. Springer, Boston, MA (2007). doi:10.1007/978-0-387-72367-9_34
13. Trivellato, D., Zannone, N., Glaundrup, M., Skowronek, J., Etalle, P.S.: A semantic security framework for systems of systems. Int. J. Coop. Inf. Syst. **22**, 1–35 (2013)
14. Becker, M., Sewell, P.: Cassandra: distributed access control policies with tunable expressiveness. In: Proceedings of the Fifth IEEE International Workshop on Policies for Distributed Systems and Networks. POLICY 2004, pp. 159–168, June 2004
15. Czenko, M., Doumen, J., Etalle, S.: Trust management in P2P systems using standard TuLiP. In: Karabulut, Y., Mitchell, J., Herrmann, P., Jensen, C.D. (eds.) IFIPTM 2008. ITIFIP, vol. 263, pp. 1–16. Springer, Boston, MA (2008). doi:10.1007/978-0-387-09428-1_1
16. Li, N., Mitchell, J., Winsborough, W.: Design of a role-based trust-management framework. In: Proceedings of the 2002 IEEE Symposium on Security and Privacy, pp. 114–130 (2002)
17. Nejdl, W., Olmedilla, D., Winslett, M.: PeerTrust: automated trust negotiation for peers on the semantic web. In: Jonker, W., Petković, M. (eds.) SDM 2004. LNCS, vol. 3178, pp. 118–132. Springer, Heidelberg (2004). doi:10.1007/978-3-540-30073-1_9
18. Lampe, T.A., Prasse, C., Diefenbach, A., Ginzler, T., Sliwa, J., McLaughlin, S.: TACTICS TSI Architecture. In: International Conference on Military Communications and Information Systems ICMCIS (2016)
19. Gkioulos, V., Flizikowski, A., Stachowicz, A., Nogalski, D., Gleba, K., Sliwa, J.: Interoperability of security and quality of service policies over tactical SOA. Submitted for review at: Military Communication conference-MILCOM (2016)
20. NATO: Nato c3 classification taxonomy, March 2012. https://www.act.nato.int/article-8a
21. Baader, F., Calvanese, D., McGuinness, D.L., Nardi, D., Patel-Schneider, P.F. (eds.): The Description Logic Handbook: Theory, Implementation, and Applications. Cambridge University Press, New York (2003)

# Physical Attestation and Authentication to Detect Cheating in Resource Constrained Smart Micro-grids

Pacome L. Ambassa[1]([✉]), Stephen D. Wolthusen[2,3], Anne V.D.M. Kayem[1], and Christoph Meinel[4]

[1] Department of Computer Science, University of Cape Town,
Rondebosch 7701, Cape Town, South Africa
{pambassa,akayem}@cs.uct.ac.za
[2] Norwegian Information Security Laboratory,
Norwegian University of Science and Technology, Gjøvik, Norway
[3] School of Mathematics and Information Security, Royal Holloway,
University of London, London, UK
stephen.wolthusen@rhul.ac.uk
[4] Hasso Plattner Institute, University of Potsdam, Potsdam, Germany
meinel@hpi.de

**Abstract.** We present a physical attestation and authentication approach to detecting cheating in resource constrained smart micro-grids. A multi-user smart micro-grid (SMG) architecture supported by a low cost and unreliable communications network, forms our application scenario. In this scenario, a malicious adversary can cheat by manipulating the measured power consumption/generation data. In doing so, the reward is access to more than the per user allocated power quota. Cheating discourages user participation and results in grid destabilisation and a breakdown of the grid in the worst case. Detecting cheating attacks is thus essential for secure and resilient SMG management, but is also a challenging problem. We address this problem with a cheating detection scheme that integrates the idea of *physical attestation* and *authentication via on control signals* to assess whether or not the SMG system is under attack. A theoretical analysis demonstrates the efficiency and correctness of our proposed scheme for constrained SMGs.

**Keywords:** Smart micro-grid · Replay attacks · Data injection · Power consumption misreporting · Critical infrastructure · Lossy networks

## 1 Introduction

A stand-alone constrained smart micro-grid (SMG) is an intelligent and a cost-effective power sharing solution aimed at ensuring reliable access to electrical power in impoverished energy communities that are not connected to the national power grid [1]. SMGs are self-contained cyber-physical energy-based systems (CPS) which integrate cyber (information technology) systems with the physical system (Power network) for sensing, computation, communication, and control to deliver energy with greater efficiency,

© Springer International Publishing AG 2017
N. Cuppens-Boulahia et al. (Eds.): CyberICPS 2016, LNCS 10166, pp. 52–68, 2017.
DOI: 10.1007/978-3-319-61437-3_4

reliability, and security. In the SMG, the power sharing infrastructure is supported by small-scale distributed energy resources (DER), based on renewable sources of energy such as photovoltaic panels and wind turbines that are intermittent and volatile.

An efficient energy management mechanism is, therefore, critical to balancing demand and supply to/from DERs. The SMG relies on sensors, metering devices, and advanced communication networking infrastructure for control and monitoring. On the one hand, monitoring is useful for collecting measurement data distributed over the network. On the other hand, control involves analysing the data (drawn from monitoring). Both monitoring and control are therefore essential for supporting multiple activities such as ensuring grid stability, detecting cheating or data distortions, load forecasting, facilitating demand response and preventing disruption.

The standard smart grid (SG) architecture relies on a centralised Supervisory Control and Data Acquisition (SCADA) system and an Advanced Metering Infrastructure (AMI) composed of highly calibrated, trustworthy sensors such as phasor measurement units (PMUs), smart meters (SMs), and an extensive communication infrastructure. Due to their high cost, SMs and PMUs are not likely to be used in constrained SMGs. In resource constrained SMGs, however, for economic reasons, monitoring and control operations can be supported by an insecure and unreliable network [2]. This however implies that the devices that underlie the network are not tamper-resistant. Furthermore, in certain cases, usability designs place device control solely on the user-end. Thus, attacks centred on cheating are a serious concern, since cheating attacks[1] can in the long-term lead to grid destabilisation. Accurate monitoring is therefore vital to reliable and trustworthy grid operation.

To this end, we specifically investigate two types of cheating attacks in this paper, namely: **Replay** and **Random Data Perturbation** attacks. Both attacks are easier to provoke on SMGs than on standard SG architectures. In the case of **replay attacks**, the adversary aims to ensure that the data modifications are unidentifiable, while in the **random data perturbation attack** case, the adversary is concerned with modifying the data before it is reported, but wishes to conceal his/her identity. We note that cheating attacks lead to issues such as false consumption reports and incorrect billing that affect data integrity. As such, this not only creates a situation of distrust but may also lead to unbalanced demand and supply, thus, affecting the stability of the SMG.

In this paper, we propose a cheating detection algorithm and a cheating identification algorithm for the SMG. The proposed scheme builds on Roth and McMillin's physical attestation proposed to detect the occurrence of cheating attacks, and uses a control signal or physical watermarking to identify the node(s) from which the attack was provoked [3–5]. The advantage of using physical attestation and control signal techniques over cryptographic-based techniques is that they are not computationally intensive, which is suitable for resource-constrained systems [6, 7]. The intuition behind this approach is to embed a secret control signal to the data stream, such that any adversarial modification (cheating) to the original data would corrupt the legitimate control signal and lead to a discrepancy between the observation at the physical layer with the reported (and possibly compromised) value. We consider a framework where both

---

[1] Cheating means that a node is reporting a value that is different from what is reflective on the power network to achieves malicious goal.

cyber and physical infrastructures are modelled as graphs with different topologies sharing nodes. The data model is organised in the form of overlapping clusters, such that all cluster nodes have shared knowledge of the control signal and report data by our protocol specifications. Adversarial nodes, have no knowledge of the shared control signal and so report data differently from expected. We extend Roth and McMillin's physical attestation scheme [8] to detect multiple cheating nodes based on the so called group attestation. More specifically, the network is divided into a set of partitions. Each partition aggregates data and compares the data from the cyber layer to the physical layer. In addition, inter-node trust, within a subgraph (partition), is established by adding a secret control signal to reported consumption values. This control signal is kept secret from the attacker.

The rest of the paper is organized as follows. Section 2 briefly reviews the literature on data integrity attacks and countermeasures. In Sect. 3, we describe our proposed SMG model and follow this in Sect. 4 with a definition of our cheating attack model. Section 5 provides a detection framework and also presents our cheating detection and identification schemes. We provide a performance and correctness analysis in Sect. 6 and conclude in Sect. 7.

## 2  Related Work

Data modification attacks in smart grids, fall under the general area of deception attacks in which the adversary's goal is to compromise data integrity. Typical deception attacks distort price signals and data measurements. Liu *et al.* [9], described a variant of deception attacks in which the adversary uses network knowledge to modify state estimations stealthily. These false data injection attacks (FDIAs) are not detectable by existing bad measurement detection algorithms and can induce the control centre into making decisions that affect power flow and marketing schemes negatively. Qin *et al.* [10] address this problem with the concept of unidentifiable attacks as a more practical adversarial strategy for attackers with limited resources. The unidentifiable attack in contrast to FDIA enables the attacker to compromise a set of smart meters and inject false data. In this case, the control system can indicate that the system is under attacks but cannot deterministically deduce which nodes or set of smart meters have been compromised. Many FDIA detection methods in centralised and decentralised systems have been proposed including statistical test [11], machine learning based approach [12,13], Watermarking techniques [14] and short-term forecasting methods [15]. However, most of these works do not consider limited computational capability networks.

Mo and Sinopoli [3] introduced the problem of detecting replay attacks in control systems and developed a detection approach based on the injection of a secret a Gaussian white noise signal to the control input and test the estimation residue for the output estimation error of the Kalman filter. Assuming that the added white noise is known to the controller, a $\chi^2$ detector is then used to detect the presence of the replay attack. When there is no attack, the added white noise is removed with the Kalman filter. Further extensions [4,5], add a physical watermarking secret signal to the control signal so that under normal conditions, the controller should be able to detect the presence of the watermark in the sensor measurements. The watermark plays the role of an authenticator and follows a Gaussian distribution with zero means. Although this solution works on the control system, it is less suitable for an SMG. Tran *et al.* [16], use the same solution approach, but instead add Gaussian noise periodically making it difficult for the adversary to emulate noise addition patterns accurately.

Roth and McMillin [8], proposed addressing this issue by using the physical invariants to detect data falsifications. However, the Roth and McMillin scheme has two limitations: first, it considers a SMG as a static system, and second, the approach is limited to single attack detection on linear physical topologies which is not effective for a resource constrained SMG.

We recall that the efficiency of the detection mechanism is integral to guaranteeing user trust and consequently micro-grid stability. Therefore, an efficient multi-node cheating detection scheme is a good way of preventing cheating on resource constrained SMG with stochastic power fluctuations. We are now ready to, first of all, describe the fundamentals of our system model and then proceed to describe the cheating and detection models.

## 3   System Model

A SMG can be modelled as a distributed system integrating DERs such as wind turbines and solar panels, supporting local demands and a lossy communication network to facilitate reliable power sharing in rural and remote areas that are difficult or expensive to connect to standard power grid architectures. The SMG model as proposed in [2,17] consists of power and data network, structured as a decentralised system composed of some buses, power lines, household or nodes, distributed energy resources (DER). The SMG consists of a set of $N$ consumers (or households or nodes) denoted as $C = c_1, ..., c_N$. The SMG is designed in such a way that a subset of consumers, namely prosumers, shared energy produced among the neighbour's households through connecting links in a tree architecture.

The power network is based on Direct Current (DC) and can be represented by an undirected connected graph where nodes and edges represent consumers and connecting links. A supply node has an energy consumption that is less than the energy it generates; the reverse is true for a demand node. The nodes (supply or demand) are connected by connecting lines (branches). We assume that supply nodes share power with a set of demand households which are connected to the distribution line. However, not every household is connected to a single branch (parallel); some households may, for instance, share the same branch (series).

The data network can be summarised as a three-layered heterogeneous network. The lower layer consists of the *household network* where sensor nodes measure generation/consumption data and communicate to the reporting device (mobile devices) acting as intermediate data collectors. The second layer is in the *neighbourhood network* where one or more households are grouped in a cluster connected with the data aggregators/concentrators. Finally, the third layer is the *aggregation network* between the several data aggregators and utility centre. Data aggregator collects and aggregates measurements from a cluster of consumers, process the measurements and forwards the aggregated data to the control centre through networks. The information is processed and analysed at the data aggregator (as it is assumed to have sufficient computation capabilities) before being further transmitted to the control centre for further processing, analysis and billing purposes. Moreover, the collected data can also be forwarded to other aggregators to which they are densely interconnected via a mesh network to minimise the risk of lost data.

As the system is heterogeneous, several types of communications technology can be used between the different types of nodes. The communications media between the sensor node, mobile phone, and aggregator is primarily wireless (Bluetooth, ZigBee, WiFi) while communication between the data aggregator and the utility provider is based on cellular networks. In this paper, we only focus on the communication between the reporting device at the household and the aggregation node. Such nodes communicate by message passing. The nodes communicate with each other directly when in wireless communication range, otherwise, the message is transmitted via multi-hop routes in which intermediate nodes act as routing nodes. We assume that each cluster has a unique cluster ID, and each node has a unique node ID. We assume that sensors and mobiles devices that forward measurement reports have a limited computation and communication capability and can be compromised by the adversary.

For simplicity, as a first solution step, we design our model on the assumption that the underlying communication protocol is fault-free and can provide reliable communication (overcome transient communications failures). The system is asynchronous, which means that there are no bounds on the processing times or communication delays. This assumption means that the messages may be delayed and may be delivered in a different order than the one in which they were sent. Every node in the SMG Network has an associated address. This is used during network communication to identify the nodes individually.

We consider that time is divided into a period denoted $\mathcal{T}$. Every $k\mathcal{T}$th reporting period $[k\mathcal{T}, (k + 1)\mathcal{T}]$ a snapshot algorithm is regularly used to collect a stream of data from the consumer household [2].

We define $I_{c_i}(k)$, $V_{c_i}(k)$ and $P_{c_i}(k)$ the current, the voltage magnitudes and the power respectively from node $c_i$ in the $k$th reporting period. We define $X_{c_i}(k)$ the vector containing the measurement from consumer $c_i$ at the $k$th reporting period. $X_{c_i}(k)$ can be a multidimensional vector with $X_{c_i}(k) = [I_{c_i}(k), V_{c_i}(k), P_{c_i}(k)]$. The measurements from the sensors collected by the consumer $c_i$ are assumed to be bounded between a minimum and a maximum values, $\forall k, X_{c_i}(k) \in [X_{c_i}^{\min}, X_{c_i}^{\max}]$. We define $Y_{c_i}(k)$ the authenticated measurements from $c_i$ that is communicated to the data aggregator. $Y_{c_i}(k)$ consists in embedding a secret control signal (watermark) $C_{c_i}(k)$ chosen by $c_i$ to $X_{c_i}(k)$. Here $C_{c_i}(k)$ represents the secret control signal. Each node $c_i$, reports the measurements in the form of the message $M_{c_i}(k)$ described as follows:

$$M_{c_i}(k) = ID_{c_i} \| Y_{c_i}(k) \tag{1}$$

where $ID_{c_i}$ represents the sender's ID node and $Y_{c_i}(k)$ the modified measurement.

## 4   Cheating Attack Model

Our cheating model is focused on the cheater who is internal to the SMG and whose goal is to obtain financial gain. We assume that the cheater's goal is solely to manipulate the system into behaving in a way that benefits the cheater (e.g. subverting power consumption fees). We assume a limited adversary having only partial knowledge of the network topology and/or power consumption patterns. This is mostly due to the dynamic nature of the network. On the other hand, we consider that a cheater can compromise a limited number of metering devices, and has the capability to inject false data via the compromised component not only once but over the different reporting period.

In our cheating model, the adversary compromises reporting devices at the household level and reports bad data to the aggregator node. We assume that the utility centre and aggregator nodes are trustworthy and cannot be compromised. Finally, we assume that communication links are secure, this because they are protected by some security mechanisms such as authentication and encryption (symmetric encryption protocol). We assume that our SMG is failure-free and as such, messages that are sent, eventually reach the destination without being modified or dropped by the communication medium. However, since no other security mechanism is running on the metering devices, we consider tampering with the measurement devices as a viable form of attack.

Our solution model allows attacks to be provoked as individual isolated events to minimise the risk of the attacker being discovered. Two major types of attacks are considered:

**Replay Attacks (RAs).** RA, as defined in the traditional security system, are simple attacks where an attacker records an arbitrary number of measurements and proceeds by reordering the time stamps in such a way to mimic the sequence of new timestamps.

More formally, consider $C = c_1, ..., c_N$ the set of consumers and $Y_{c_i}(k)$ the authenticated measurement vector reported by consumer $c_i$ at the $k$th reporting period. Now suppose that the attacker has recorded data during an number of periods and that at a given attack interval say $k_a$, replays the recorded data instead of reporting the new power measurement value. The attacker then modifies the time interval associated with the measurements so as to induce the device into reporting a modified value $\hat{Y}_{c_i}(k)$ as follows:

$$\hat{Y}_{c_i}(k) = \begin{cases} Y_{c_i}(k) & \text{for } k \notin k_a \\ Y_{c_i}(k - \xi) & \text{for } k \in k_a \end{cases} \tag{2}$$

where $k_a$ denotes the attack interval and $\xi$ is a positive integer($\xi > 0$).

Mo and Sinopoli [3] have proven that under the replay attack the measurements residuals [11] will converge to the same distribution as $Y_{c_i}(k)$. Thus making the conventional $\chi^2$ detector not suitable for replay attack detection.

**Random Data Perturbation Attack (RDPA).** A RDPA, works by enabling an attacker to manipulate the consumption data by creating random variations in household power data. An attacker could lower or increase the reported energy measurement to cause disruptions. Power data manipulations could result in unstable operation of the SMG [18]. The strategy to provoke the RDPA is for the adversary to modify the power consumption data before the consumer reports it. The attackers have access to the measurements and can modify the values to be reported by adding an attack vector in such a way that the device reports the following values:

$$\hat{Y}_{c_i}(k) = \begin{cases} Y_{c_i}(k) & \text{for} \quad k \notin k_a \\ Y_{c_i}(k) + \gamma_{c_i}(k) & \text{for} \quad k \in k_a \end{cases} \qquad (3)$$

Where $Y_{c_i}(k)$ is the modified data transmitted by the consumer household $c_i$ and $\gamma_{c_i}(k)$ is an arbitrary nonzero value introduce by the attacker to form $\hat{Y}_{c_i}(k)$.

We assume that at least one of the cheating attacks mentioned above is provoked. A cheating attack detection mechanism is therefore needed to counter such attacks. The detection scheme works by partitioning the nodes into clusters $S_i$ such that each of the clusters is organised to ensure that the nodes are grouped into disjoint sets.

## 5   Cheating Detection Scheme

In this section, we propose a scheme to detect the cheating attacks detailed in Sect. 4. We assume a particular SMG model where the power and data networks are modelled as two separate graphs sharing vertices, denoted $(\mathcal{V}, \mathcal{Y})$ and $(\mathcal{V}, \mathcal{Q})$ respectively.

The power network is graphically represented by $(\mathcal{V}, \mathcal{Y})$ where nodes or vertices correspond to supply and demand nodes or both and edges correspond to branches $\mathcal{Y} \subseteq \mathcal{J} \times \mathcal{J}$. While the data network $(\mathcal{V}, \mathcal{Q})$, where $\mathcal{V}$ is the vertex set (each vertex or node corresponds either to a consumer reporting devices or a data concentrator) and $\mathcal{Q}$ is the set of edges, corresponding to the links (hop) between two vertices. Undirected edges are represented by the commutativity law as follows $\{x, y\} = \{y, x\}$, and $\{x, y\} \in \mathcal{Q}$ means that nodes $x$ and $y$ are adjacent if there is a direct link between $x$ and $y$, i.e. they are within mutual transmission range. We represent the set of neighbours (adjacent nodes) of $x$ by $N(x) = \{y | \{x, y\} \in \mathcal{Q}\}$.

We model the SMG as a joint of the two networks to form $\mathcal{G} = (\mathcal{V}, \mathcal{E})$ where $\mathcal{V}$ is the vertex set (each vertex or node corresponds either to a supply node or demand node in power network; or consumer reporting devices/a data concentrator in communication network) and $\mathcal{E} = \mathcal{Y} \cup \mathcal{Q}$ is the set of edges, corresponding to either the links (hop) or branches connecting two vertices.

The design of the detection framework, is based on the principles of *divide-and-conquer* [19]. The graph $\mathcal{G} = (\mathcal{V}, \mathcal{E})$ is partitioned into an interconnected set of sub-graphs (also referred to as clusters) of arbitrary sizes. The motivation behind this is that partitioning the graph helps to perform a limited number of tests (for cheating detection) in each partition, which is a more efficient procedure than performing tests on the whole system. We make the assumption that the partitions are organised such that the power network at each sub-graph (cluster) is independent, but the communication networks overlap. For any link connecting two nodes in the power network, there is also a corresponding path in the communication network. As such the start and end nodes are the same in both networks, but the intermediate nodes are different. The nodes in the power network are connected both in series and parallel, and are both connected to the data concentrator. Each cluster, for instance, could be composed of multiple consumer households representing different nodes.

Our solution approach presented in this paper relyies on the assumption that the set of nodes in $\mathcal{G}$ is partitioned into overlapping sub-graphs (clusters). This can be achieved for instance, by adding the overlapping constraint in the neighbourhood network [2].

We consider a scenario with a set of $p$ sub-graph (cluster) denoted $S_1, S_2, ..., S_p$, where $1 \leq i \leq p$, such that, $\forall S_i : \mathcal{V}_i \neq \emptyset$. Several of these subsets overlap i.e. $\forall (i, k) \in 1, .., p$, $i \neq k$, $S_i \cap S_k \neq \emptyset$. The union of $\mathcal{V}_i$ is equal to $\mathcal{V}$ where $\bigcup_{1 \leq i \leq p} \mathcal{V}_i = \mathcal{V}(\mathcal{G})$. Each node is assumed to belong to more than one cluster. How the nodes are partitioned is considered out of the scope of this paper.

This assumption is formally stated in Definition 1 below.

**Definition 1.** *Let $S_i = (\mathcal{V}_i, \mathcal{E}_i)$ and $S_k = (\mathcal{V}_k, \mathcal{E}_k)$ be a set of clusters on $\mathcal{G}$, we say that there is a set of vertices $x, y \in \mathcal{V}_i, \mathcal{V}_k$ respectively, where $1 \leq i, k \leq p$, such that $\forall i, k : \exists x \in \mathcal{V}_i, y \in \mathcal{V}_k : ((x, y) \in \mathcal{V}(\mathcal{G}) \wedge (x, y) \in \mathcal{V}_i \wedge (x, y) \notin \mathcal{V}_k)).$*

Cluster nodes are ordered by a tree topology to facilitate data exchange, with the root of the tree represented by a data concentrator or aggregator that collects and analyses data to ensure conformance to accepted thresholds before transmission to the utility centre for demand response. The data aggregator (data concentrator), is also assumed to be connected to a generator and supplies the network with power. We further assume that a trusted measurement of the power consumed can be obtained from this node, thus making it the ***entry point*** for the power network at the cluster level from 'which power is supplied through the physical lines branching into the households and eventually the electrical appliances.

## 5.1   Attack Detection and Node Identification

Resilience to cheating is essential to SMG trust and stability. In this section, we propose a low-cost and efficient solution to cheating in the SMGs. Our goal is to detect cheating attacks and identify compromised nodes using the attack detection scheme. More specifically, each node in a given partition will generate a control signal. The secret control signal is embedded in the measured power consumption value to be reported and therefore modifies the power consumption by a particular amount that is secret to the attacker. The authenticated measurements data are then transmitted to the data aggregator. Upon reception of the data, the data aggregator combines the power data reported. A correlation test is then used to confirm that the received measurements (aggregated) are consistent with the physical invariants of the system.

As mentioned earlier, the detection approach is based on two principals components, namely, the control signal (CS) and the physical attestation (PA). CS is a secret signal added to the reported data for authentication, while the PA is used to compare the reported data with the estimated data from physical invariants.

## 5.2   Control Signal Design

We design the CS or watermark signal by considering that in each cluster, the reporting node generates a CS (key) that is embedded to the power consumption/generation measurements before transmission. However, sharing a particular control signal beforehand can be energy-consuming task, as the operation can imply the exchange of several messages. A simple approach is either to enable each node to generate a random value or to enable the data aggregator to dictate a specific value to each cluster member.

We use a random approach and design a CS as a vector of real values that is independent of the measurement errors. The CS is generated at each reporting period i.e. at each time slot $k$, a management device at node $c_i \in S_i$ generates a IID Pseudo-Random Number Generator (PRNG). As noted by Bhattarai et al. [14] we assume that mobile device contains a pre-programmed function when manufactured. The function takes as input the measurement data and a pre-shared secret key [20]; and the output is the data with CS embedded. The generated CS is embedded to $X_{c_i}(k)$ and the resulting value $Y_{c_i}(k) = X_{c_i}(k) + C_{c_i}(k)$ is transmitted to the data aggregator. We assume that freshness of the CS is ensured by a mechanism that reduces the correlation between the CS at different periods [4,5]. Specifically the CS is randomly generated, such that:

$$\sum_{c_i \in S_i} X_{c_i}(k) \approx \sum_{c_i \in S_i} (X_{c_i}(k) + C_{c_i}(k)) \tag{4}$$

Where $C_{c_i}(k)$ is the randomly generated CS and $X_{c_i}(k)$ represents the power measurements. The above equation can also be expressed as:
$\sum_{c_i \in S_i} X_{c_i}(k) = \sum_{c_i \in S_i} (X_{c_i}(k) + C_{c_i}(k)) - \epsilon(k)$, where $\epsilon(k)$ is the error obtained by adding random numbers. $\epsilon$ is the sum of all added random values: $\epsilon = \sum_{c_i \in S_i} C_{c_i}(k)$.

### 5.3 Physical Attestation and Conservation of Energy

Cyber-Physical attestation is a trust establishment mechanism that allows a system to attest their state to an external verifier. CPS attestation enables the verifier to monitor the physic of system to detect attacks [7]. In order to use PA, one must consider a trusted verifier, having a correct view of how the system should behave. In SG application scenario, Roth and McMillin [8] specify that before using PA, a set of physical invariants must be defined. An invariant is a logical assertion that must remain true during system execution. In a SMG, invariants are laws that must hold due to the physics of the system. PA uses a set of invariants that evaluate to either true or false to determine if a portion of the system has been compromised. The theory behind this invariant approach is that a physical law cannot be violated by the physical system. Falsifications can only occur when instantiations have been made with bad measurements. The set of violated invariants is then used to determine which of the nodes provided the falsified measurements.

In this work, we build on Roth and McMillin's approach to consider the PA of a set of data originating from several nodes in the partition $S_i$. The trustworthy verifier, namely the aggregator, knows the topology of the power network in the partition. Based on the connectivity of the different nodes, the verifier considers Kirchoff's and Ohm's Law; and the conservation of power of the physical system to detect cheating.

We define $P_{c_i}(k)$ the power at $c_i$. $P_{c_i}(k)$ is expressed as $P_{c_i}(k) = Gen_{c_i}(k) - Load_{c_i}(k)$, where $Gen_{c_i}(k)$ and $Load_{c_i}(k)$ are the generation amount and the load at node $c_i$ on the $k$th time period.

The power network is composed of a set of nodes and power supply lines connecting these nodes. The lines connecting the nodes represent the distribution lines, also called branches. Multiple branches can connect two nodes either in series or parallel.

Let $\mathcal{V}$ denote the collection of all nodes. Each line connects a pair of nodes $c_i, c_j$. Let $\mathcal{E}$ denotes the collection of all lines. For each node $c_i$, let $V_{c_i}(k)$ denote its voltage,

$I_{c_i}(k)$ denote its current injection, and $P_{c_i}(k)$ denote its power. For each line connecting $c_i, c_j$, let $I_{c_i c_j}(k)$ denote the current flowing from node $c_i$ to node $c_j$ in a DC network.

For simplicity, the generators are assumed to be an ***ideal current source*** and have no losses. We assume that measurements at the data concentrator are trusted and consider the data concentrator as the entry point from which branches to the various nodes (households) can be made. Given the measurements of the electric current and voltage at the entry point and supply nodes, our objective is to estimate the electric current and voltages at each line segment between consumer $c_i$ to the data concentrator.

The power flow is formulated both at the node level or the branches. At each node, the voltage magnitude is evaluated on the branches, the currents, and powers flowing on the branches is evaluated.

On the other hand, current and power flow can be modelled according to node connectivity. We consider two case scenarios: in the first, all the nodes (supply and demand) are connected to the same line segment (connected in series) [8]. This is also equivalent to connecting the components sequentially.

The line segment (branch) between the data concentrator and the consumer $c_j$ contains $e$ nodes connected in series such that $m$ are supply nodes and $e - m$ are demands node. The supply nodes are assumed to have positive current injections denoted $I_s$ while the demand nodes are assumed to have negative current injections denoted $I_l$. By the law of conservation of energy, the sum of the current injected into the node must equal the sum of the currents emitted from the node to ensure an equilibrium.

$$\sum_{s=1}^{m} I_s = \sum_{l=1}^{e-m} I_l \tag{5}$$

The current flowing between node $c_i$ and node $c_j$, denoted $I_{c_i c_j}(k)$ is given by

$$I_{c_i c_j}(k) = \frac{V_{c_i}(k) - V_{c_j}(k)}{R_{c_i c_j}(k)} \tag{6}$$

According to Kirchoff's current law, $I_{c_i}(k)$ is equal the algebraic sum of the currents flowing away from node $c_i$:

$$I_{c_i}(k) = \sum_{c_i \neq c_j} I_{c_i c_j}(k) = \sum_{c_i \neq c_j} \frac{V_{c_i}(k) - V_{c_j}(k)}{R_{c_i c_j}(k)} \tag{7}$$

Moreover, the power $P_{c_i}(k)$ consumed or produced at the node $c_i$ is represented by:

$$P_{c_i}(k) = Gen_{c_i}(k) - Load_{c_i}(k) = V_{c_i}(k) \times I_{c_i}(k) \tag{8}$$

In the second, the case of multiple consumers connected to different line segments in parallel, $R_{c_i c_j}(k)$, represents the link resistance on the branch connecting $c_i$ and $c_j$ while $V_{c_i}(k)$ and $V_{c_j}(k)$ are the respective voltage magnitudes at nodes $c_i$ and $c_j$. We can therefore use Ohm's law to express the corresponding current and voltage flows between any two nodes $c_i$, and $c_j$, in the power network, as follows:

$$\sum_{c_i \neq c_j} V_{c_i}(k) - V_{c_j}(k) = \sum_{c_i \neq c_j} I_{c_i c_j}(k) R_{c_i c_j}(k) \tag{9}$$

In addition to the above, we make the following assumptions about the underlying structure of our network.

- The topology of the (power) network is known and stable for the duration of measurements
- Each aggregator knows the power network's topology, it can obtain power injected at each node and estimate power flowing between nodes. It is further assumed that each aggregator employs physical invariants build from conservation of energy and laws of electricity.
- For the message exchange, our underlying communication network is asynchronous and fault free. These are the necessary prerequisites for reliable ordered multicast protocols [21, Chap. 15] to ensure reliability and preserve message ordering. Reliability ensures that message ordering obeys the sequence of emission (first-in-first-out (FIFO)) order
- The ID denoted $ID_{c_i}$ of the sender's node is associated with each message and can directly be linked to the node.

## 5.4   Detection of Cheating Attacks

The main idea behind the detection approach is to compute the aggregation of data collected in each partition (cluster) via a spanning tree and then allow the aggregation node to verify the aggregate value and test whether or not a cheating attack has occurred. The aggregator compares the aggregated measurements values transmitted by the nodes belonging to the cluster to the expected measurements estimated from the physical properties of the system. The aggregator detects cheating if there is a strong inconsistency between the aggregate value received and the expected. However, the cheating detection approach developed herein only helps in detecting the occurrence of a cheating attack but, neither help in determining when the cheating had occurred, i.e. if you are cheating right now or whether you were behaving correctly when the measurement was performed, nor consider the problem of identifying the compromised node. To overcome that limitation, the test should be repeated to reduce false positive occurrences

The cheating detection algorithm (Algorithm 1) receives as input a graph $G = (\mathcal{V}, \mathcal{E})$, a set of clusters $S_i$ and a threshold $\epsilon(k)$. The aggregator node aggregates the measurements collected at the $k$ th reporting time. Cheating detection is achieved at each aggregation point in the partition $S_i$ and the proposed cheating detection algorithm (Algorithm 1) consists of three stages. In the first stage data aggregator nodes queries each consumer households (Initialisation). In the second stage, namely **collection and aggregation** each consumer household node transmits the data collected during that time interval to the aggregator for aggregation. The third, **verification and attestation** stage, serves to verify that the aggregation of the reported measurements corresponds to the expected measurements.

**Initialisation.** The Initialisation consists of the data aggregator $AggS_i$ to querying the nodes in the partition by broadcasting a request for data collection from $c_i \in S_i$.

**Collection and Aggregation.** The second stage namely, collection and aggregation is subdivided into of three steps. In the first step each node $c_i \in S_i$ upon reception of the request, chooses a secret random CS $C_{c_i}(k)$ (see Sect. 5.2). Then adds $C_{c_i}(k)$ to the measurements vectors $X_{c_i}(k)$ and obtains the modified value $Y_{c_i}(k) = X_{c_i}(k) + C_{c_i}(k)$. In the second step, $c_i \in S_i$ transmits the resulting $Y_{c_i}(k)$ to the data aggregator $AggS_i$ using a multi-hop communication system. Falsified measurements values such as $\hat{Y}_{c_i}(k)$ can be reported in case of cheating attacks. Third, the aggregator, on reception of $Y_{c_i}(k)$ from $c_i$, then aggregates of the received data.

**Verification and Attestation Phase.** Once the collection and aggregation phases are completed, the trusted data aggregator detect cheating on the aggregated data based on the correlation between the reported data from a set $c_i \in S_i$ and estimated data from the DC power network. Such a verification is based on its knowledge of the power network topology and the use PA to verify the authenticity of the aggregated value. Specifically, the reported measurement value is checked for consistency with the physical obser-vation. In the case of inconsistencies between the reported aggregate values and the estimated value, the data aggregator decides whether or not cheating has occurred by comparing the difference between the two values to a threshold value. When the differ-ence surpasses $\epsilon(k)$, this indicates that there is at least one cheating node in the set of reporting nodes. Otherwise, the reported data are considered good and are then used for further analysis and state estimation. To evaluate the difference between the two values, we employ a simple distance metric that reflects similarity in time [22]. Specifically, if the two measurements data are similar, they will exhibit a low distance from each other; otherwise, they exhibit high distance from each other, thus low similarity. The detection of the cheating attack is done by computing the distance between the sum of reported measurements and the estimated physical values and comparing such a distance with the threshold value. Let $Z_{c_i}(k)$ be a vector with the sum of estimated physical value. An attack exist if:

$$\left| \sum_{c_i \in S_i} Y_{c_i}(k) - \sum_{c_i \in S_i} Z_{c_i}(k) \right| > \epsilon(k) \tag{10}$$

We define $\epsilon(k)$ as the distance between the measurement $Y_{c_i}(k)$ reported at the $k$th period using the communication system and $Z_{c_i}(k)$ the sum based on the power flow invariant at the same reporting period is given by:

$$\left| \sum_{c_i \in S_i} (X_{c_i}(k) + \sum_{c_i \in S_i} C_{c_i}(k)) - \sum_{c_i \in S_i} Z_{c_i}(k) \right| > \epsilon(k) \tag{11}$$

The attestation is based on the notion of **group attestation** where the attestation is made at the aggregator node, but the process depends on a physical path between the aggregation node and a reporting node (in the group sub-tree). More specifically, the group attestation is based on the network connectivity and considers that the node can be connected either in series or in parallel.

Once the cheating is detected i.e. the Algorithm 1 returns $Detection(S_i) = True$, the following step is the identification of the cheating node.

---

**Algorithm 1.** Cheating Attack Detection

---

1   **Input:** A graph $G = (V, \mathcal{E})$, a set of cluster $S_i$ and a threshold $\epsilon(k) \in$
    **Output:** A boolean stating if cheating has occurred or not

2   $Detection(S_i) = False$ /* First stage: Initialisation            */

3   **foreach** $S_i$ **do**

4       $Aggs_i$ broadcasts a request to aggregation

5       Waits for response from the node in $S_i$
       /* Second stage: Collection and aggregation       */

6       $Aggs_i$ get $I_{c_i}(k)$

7       $Aggs_i$ get $V_{c_i}(k)$

8       $Aggs_i$ get $P_{c_i}(k)$

9       $Aggs_i$ get $P_{c_i c_j}(k)$

10      **for** $c_i \in S_i$ **do**

11          Once $c_i \in S_i$ received request from $Aggs_i$

12          $Detection(S_i) \leftarrow False$

13          $Detection(S_i) \leftarrow False$

14          **if** $k \notin k_a$ **then**

15             $M_{c_i}(k) = ID_{c_i} \| Y_{c_i}(k)$

16             $c_i \in S_i$ sends $M_{c_i}(k) = ID_{c_i} \| Y_{c_i}(k)$ to $Aggs_i$

17          **else if** $k \in k_a$ **then**

18             $\hat{Y}_{c_i}(k) \begin{cases} Y_{c_i}(k) + \gamma_{c_i}(k) & \text{/* RDPA */} \\ Y_{c_i}(k - \xi) & \text{/* RA */} \end{cases} \quad M_{c_i}(k) = ID_{c_i} \| \hat{Y}_{c_i}(k)$

19             $c_i \in S_i$ sends $M_{c_i}(k) = ID_{c_i} \| \hat{Y}_{c_i}(k)$ to $Aggs_i$

20      **if** $Aggs_i$ receives $M_{c_i}(k)$ **then**

21          $Aggs_i$ Computes $\sum_{c_i \in S_i} Y_{c_i}(k) = \sum_{c_i \in S_i} Y_{c_i}(k) + \sum_{c_i \in S_i} C_{c_i}(k)$
     /* Third stage: Verification and attestation phase     */

22      **for** $c_i \in S_i$ **do**

23          **if** $\left| \sum_{c_i \in S_i} Y_{c_i}(k) - \sum_{c_i \in S_i} Z_{c_i}(k) \right| > \epsilon(k)$ **then**

24             $Detection(S_i) \leftarrow True$

25          **else**

26             $Detection(S_i) \leftarrow False$

---

### 5.5 Compromised Node Identification

We have a non-anonymous system where each message exchanged is considered to be unique. This is to say that the unique identifier of a node is associated with the messages. Such identifier can be directly linked to the node from whom it is originating. When dealing with cheating, it is not enough to detect the attacks, but it is also important to identify the node where the modification has taken place. The node misreporting is not necessarily the cheater because the adversary can inject false data into the network via compromised neighbouring metering devices.

Since the secret CS is known to the data aggregator beforehand, the aggregator attempts to verify whether the received CS is authentic. Compromised nodes are then identified, by conducting a test to check whether or not the CS associated with the reported data is authentic. This is because any malicious modification of the original data would corrupt the CS. Additionally, since the ID is associated with the node, this helps to pinpoint the compromised node. A simple verification procedure is described in [23] as a binary function $g$ with $Y_{c_i}(k)$ and $C_{c_i}(k)$ as inputs. The reported data $Y_{c_i}(k)$ from $c_i$ is authentic if $g(Y_{c_i}(k), C_{c_i}(k)) = 1$, and inauthentic if $g(Y_{c_i}(k), C_{c_i}(k)) = 0$.

Once cheating is detected in a particular round, we employ Algorithm 2, described below to identify the cheating nodes.

---

**Algorithm 2.** Compromised Node Identification

---

**Input:** $G = (V, E)$, sub-graph $S_i$ and $M_{c_i}(k)$
**Output:** The ID of the node with a inauthentic CS

1  $comp_{ID} = \emptyset$
2  **while** $Detection(S_i) = True$ **do**
3      **for** $c_i \in S_i$ **do**
4        $Aggs_i$ gets $M_{c_i}(k) = ID_{c_i} \| \hat{Y}_{c_i}(k)$
5        $Aggs_i$ extracts $C_{c_i}(k)$
6        $Aggs_i$ compute $g(Y_{c_i}(k), C_{c_i}(k))$
7        **if** $g(Y_{c_i}(k), C_{c_i}(k)) = 1$ **then**
8          Reported data is authentic
9        **else if** $g(Y_{c_i}(k), C_{c_i}(k)) = 0$ **then**
10         Reported data is not authentic
11         Node $c_i$ is compromised
12         $comp_{ID} \leftarrow comp_{ID} \cup c_i$
13  **return** $comp_{ID}$

---

Once cheating is detected, the Algorithm 2 is executed by the data aggregator to identify the compromised node. The algorithm takes as input the graph $G = (V, E)$, a set of clusters $S_i$ and the message $M_{c_i}(k)$.

The Algorithm 2 is executed at the level of the data aggregation to check the integrity of the received data. The data aggregation node, extracts the secret CS associated with the received data denoted $\hat{C}_{c_i}$. Then, the secret CS generated $C_{c_i}(k)$ is compared to the extracted one $\hat{C}_{c_i}$. Consequently, the sending node is considered compromised if $C_{c_i}(k)$ is not identical to $\hat{C}_{c_i}$.

# 6  Analysis

In this paper, we only briefly outline a sketch of the correctness proof for Algorithm 1. Due to space limitation analysis of Algorithm 2 is left for future work.

We assume that at the $k$th reporting period, at least one of the cheating attacks, namely replay or random data perturbation, is launched by the adversary.

**Lemma 1.** *If the system is fault free and at least one node is maliciously replaying previous measurement, then the Algorithm 1 can detect replay attacks.*

*Proof.* By Contradiction. Consider that Algorithm 1 runs on a fault free SMG and message delivery is reliable. However, Algorithm 1 fails to detect the replay attack. Assuming that for $c_i \in S_i$ the measurement data $Y_{c_i}(k)$ reported to $Aggs_i$ are aggregated. $Aggs_i$ estimates the power from the physical system. In the case of a replay attack, we further assume that the difference between the aggregated reported value and the estimated value is higher than the threshold value $\epsilon(k)$ then the test passes and a replay attack is detected which contradicts our initial hypothesis.

**Lemma 2.** *If the system is fault free and at least measurement data reported by one node have been randomly modified, then the Algorithm 1 can detect such attacks*

*Proof.* Analogous to the proof of Lemma 1

**Theorem 1.** *If several adversaries are replaying previous measurements or randomly falsifying measurements, then Algorithm 1 can detect such attacks.*

*Proof.* By Lemmas 1 and 2, Algorithm 1 can detect a replay attack and a random data perturbation attack. Based on the Algorithm 1 strategy, it holds that Algorithm 1 detects cheating on several $c_i$, assuming that the test condition (line 15) is met.

**Lemma 3.** *If the system is fault free and the communication is reliable, then the Algorithm 1 terminates.*

*Proof.* Consider a fault free system in which Algorithm 1 runs and message delivery is reliable. The verification and attestation phase is executed when the $Aggs_i$ collects and aggregates data. Since the message delivery is reliable, data are collected and the algorithm terminates successfully.

**Complexity Analysis.** Considering the fact that Algorithm 1 is distributed. Each, reporting period, the data aggregator $Aggs_i$ sends a message to the nodes $c_i$. Upon reception of the message, each reporting node $c_i$, sends a message $M_{c_i}(k)$ to the data aggregator $Aggs_i$ via a spanning tree. Overall the total number of messages exchanged within $S_i$ at the termination of the algorithm for a SMG with $N$ nodes, distributed over $p$ clusters, is given by $\frac{2N}{p}$. Thus the message complexity is $O(N)$. So for a SMG with $p$ clusters, the message complexity is also $O(N)$.

## 7   Conclusion

In this paper, we propose a cheating attack model and a detection solution that works efficiently in resource constrained SMGs. Cheating attacks pose a threat to reliable SMG operation. We considered two classes of cheating attacks namely **Replay** and **Random Data Perturbation** attacks against the power consumption data reporting. The countermeasures consist of detecting the attacks and identifying the cheating nodes. Our cheating attack detection mechanism is based on a graph partitioning scheme in which each partition aggregates measurements at the cyber system, and these values are compared to the observation of power flow at the physical layer. Consistency discrepancies imply that the measurements have been tampered with and that the cheating nodes must be identified and excluded from the network. A performance analysis shows that our solution approach efficiently detects the cheating attacks carried out by the limited adversary, but it fails at detecting cyber-physical attacker [24]. As future work, we are extending the detection schemes to consider both cyber-physical and cooperative attacks as well as a metric to distinguishing if the bad data detected is due to faulty/malfunctioning equipment or adversarially provoked.

**Acknowledgments.** This work was partially supported by the joint SANCOOP Programme of the Research Council of Norway and the National Research Foundation of South Africa (NRF) under the NRF grant 237817 as well as the Hasso-Plattner-Institute.

# References

1. Podmore, R., Larsen, R., Louie, H., Waldron, B.: Affordable energy solutions for developing communities. In: 2011 IEEE Power and Energy Society General Meeting, pp. 1–8, July 2011
2. Ambassa, P.L., Wolthusen, S.D., Kayem, A.V., Meinel, C.: Robust snapshot algorithm for power consumption monitoring in computationally constrained micro-grids. In: 2015 IEEE Innovative Smart Grid Technologies - Asia (ISGT ASIA), pp. 1–6, November 2015
3. Mo, Y., Sinopoli, B.: Secure control against replay attacks. In: 47th Annual Allerton Conference on Communication, Control, and Computing, Allerton 2009, pp. 911–918, September 2009
4. Mo, Y., Chabukswar, R., Sinopoli, B.: Detecting integrity attacks on scada systems. IEEE Trans. Control Syst. Technol. **22**(4), 1396–1407 (2014)
5. Mo, Y., Weerakkody, S., Sinopoli, B.: Physical authentication of control systems: Designing watermarked control inputs to detect counterfeit sensor outputs. IEEE Control Syst. **35**(1), 93–109 (2015)
6. Juma, H., Kamel, I., Kaya, L.: Watermarking sensor data for protecting the integrity. In: International Conference on Innovations in Information Technology, IIT 2008, pp. 598–602, December 2008
7. Valente, J., Barreto, C., Cárdenas, A.A.: Cyber-physical systems attestation. In: Proceedings of the 2014 IEEE International Conference on Distributed Computing in Sensor Systems, DCOSS 2014, pp. 354–357. IEEE Computer Society, Washington, DC (2014)
8. Roth, T., McMillin, B.: Physical attestation of cyber processes in the smart grid. In: Luiijf, E., Hartel, P. (eds.) CRITIS 2013. LNCS, vol. 8328, pp. 96–107. Springer, Cham (2013). doi:10.1007/978-3-319-03964-0_9
9. Liu, Y., Ning, P., Reiter, M.K.: False data injection attacks against state estimation in electric power grids. In: Proceedings of the 16th ACM Conference on Computer and Communications Security, CCS 2009, pp. 21–32. ACM, New York (2009)
10. Qin, Z., Li, Q., Chuah, M.C.: Unidentifiable attacks in electric power systems. In: Proceedings of the 2012 IEEE/ACM Third International Conference on Cyber-Physical Systems, ICCPS 2012, pp. 193–202. IEEE Computer Society, Washington, DC (2012)
11. Monticelli, A.: Electric power system state estimation. Proc. IEEE **88**(2), 262–282 (2000)
12. Esmalifalak, M., Nguyen, N.T., Zheng, R., Han, Z.: Detecting stealthy false data injection using machine learning in smart grid. In: 2013 IEEE Global Communications Conference (GLOBECOM), pp. 808–813, December 2013

13. Gu, Y., Liu, T., Wang, D., Guan, X., Xu, Z.: Bad data detection method for smart grids based on distributed state estimation. In: 2013 IEEE International Conference on Communications (ICC), pp. 4483–4487, June 2013
14. Bhattarai, S., Ge, L., Yu, W.: A novel architecture against false data injection attacks in smart grid. In: 2012 IEEE International Conference on Communications (ICC), pp. 907–911, June 2012
15. Zhao, J., Zhang, G., Scala, M.L., Dong, Z.Y., Chen, C., Wang, J.: Short-term state forecasting-aided method for detection of smart grid general false data injection attacks. IEEE Trans. Smart Grid **PP**(99), 1–11 (2015)
16. Tran, T.T., Shin, O.S., Lee, J.H.: Detection of replay attacks in smart grid systems. In: 2013 International Conference on Computing, Management and Telecommunications (ComManTel), pp. 298–302, January 2013
17. Weldehawaryat, G., Wolthusen, S.: Secure distributed demand projection in micro-grids. In: Global Information Infrastructure and Networking Symposium (GIIS) 2015, pp. 1–6 (2015)
18. Costache, M., Tudor, V., Almgren, M., Papatriantafilou, M., Saunders, C.: Remote control of smart meters: Friend or foe?. In: Proceedings of the 2011 Seventh European Conference on Computer Network Defense, EC2ND 2011, pp. 49–56. IEEE Computer Society, Washington, DC (2011)
19. Yang, Y., Wang, X., Zhu, S., Cao, G.: Sdap: A secure hop-by-hop data aggregation protocol for sensor networks. In: Proceedings of the 7th ACM International Symposium on Mobile Ad Hoc Networking and Computing, MobiHoc 2006, pp. 356–367. ACM, New York (2006)
20. Jin, T., Noubir, G., Thapa, B.: Zero pre-shared secret key establishment in the presence of jammers. In: Proceedings of the Tenth ACM International Symposium on Mobile Ad Hoc Networking and Computing, MobiHoc 2009, pp. 219–228. ACM, New York (2009)
21. Ghosh, S.: Distributed Systems: An Algorithmic Approach, 2nd edn. Chapman & Hall/CRC (2014)
22. Hautamaki, V., Nykanen, P., Franti, P.: Time-series clustering by approximate prototypes. In: 19th International Conference on Pattern Recognition, ICPR 2008, pp. 1–4, December 2008
23. Fei, C., Kwong, R.H., Kundur, D.: A hypothesis testing approach to semifragile watermark-based authentication. IEEE Trans. Inf. Forensics Secur. **4**(2), 179–192 (2009)
24. Vigo, R.: The cyber-physical attacker. In: Ortmeier, F., Daniel, P. (eds.) SAFECOMP 2012. LNCS, vol. 7613, pp. 347–356. Springer, Heidelberg (2012). doi:10.1007/978-3-642-33675-1_31

# Decentralised Scheduling of Power Consumption in Micro-grids: Optimisation and Security

Goitom K. Weldehawaryat[1](✉), Pacome L. Ambassa[2], Anesu M.C. Marufu[2], Stephen D. Wolthusen[1,3], and Anne V.D.M. Kayem[2]

[1] Norwegian Information Security Laboratory,
Norwegian University of Science and Technology, Gjøvik, Norway
{goitom.weldehawaryat,stephen.wolthusen}@ntnu.no
[2] Department of Computer Science, University of Cape Town,
Rondebosch 7701, Cape Town, South Africa
{pambassa,amarufu,akayem}@cs.uct.ac.za
[3] School of Mathematics and Information Security, Royal Holloway,
University of London, London, UK

**Abstract.** We consider a micro-grid architecture that is distributed in nature and reliant on renewable energy. In standard grid architectures, demand management is handled via scheduling protocols that are centrally coordinated. Centralised approaches are however computationally intensive, thus not suited to distributed grid architectures with limited computational power. We address this problem with a decentralised scheduling algorithm. In our scheduling algorithm, the alternating direction method of multipliers (ADMM) is used to decompose the scheduling problem into smaller sub problems that are solved in parallel over local computation devices, which yields an optimal solution. We show that ADMM can be used to model a scheduling solution that handles both decentralised and fully decentralised cases. As a further step, we show that false data injection attacks can be provoked by compromising parts of the communication infrastructure or a set of computing devices. In this case, the algorithm fails to converge to an optimum or converges toward a value that lends the attacker an advantage, and impacts the scheduling scheme negatively.

**Keywords:** Micro-grid architectures · Power consumption scheduling · Distributed demand management · Energy management · Demand response · ADMM

## 1 Introduction

Micro-grids (MGs) are low-voltage energy distribution systems that consists of a variety of energy storage, generation, and management units [1]. In distributed micro-grids, power generation is reliant on distributed renewable energy sources and storage, on battery units. These micro-grid architectures are well suited to small remote communities, where connections to the national power grid are not possible due to economic reasons [1]. However, variations in generation and demand make demand management (balancing demand and supply) a challenging problem. Matching supply and demand is vital

© Springer International Publishing AG 2017
N. Cuppens-Boulahia et al. (Eds.): CyberICPS 2016, LNCS 10166, pp. 69–86, 2017.
DOI: 10.1007/978-3-319-61437-3_5

to grid stability. Power consumption scheduling can smooth the demand profiles out over time to avoid overloading. A scheduling algorithm can therefore be used to distribute power cost-effectively, encouraging users to shift heavy consumption activities to off-peak periods. For instance, instead of turning on the washing machine at a peak period (e.g. at 6pm) the user could opt to use the machine at an off-peak period (e.g. at 11am) with the added benefit of paying less per kilowatt consumed. Centralised demand management approaches have been studied but are computationally intensive and raise privacy concerns [2,3]. Furthermore, existing power scheduling solutions assume network reliability and security. Such assumptions are unrealistic in computationally limited micro-grids, where data is transmitted over insecure and unreliable networks.

We address these challenges by first formulating a theoretical framework for the operation of the micro-grid and then formulate the problem of scheduling power distribution on the micro-grid as a convex optimisation problem [4,5], where the goal is to minimize the total power consumption while maximizing the social benefit [3] of power distribution on the grid. As a next step, we propose a decentralised electricity consumption scheduling algorithm based on alternating direction method of multipliers (ADMM) [6], which has been shown to be robust for solving optimisation problems in smart grid communication networks [7,8]. This allows each user to report demands as aggregated rather than single values which addresses the privacy concern. The computational burden is alleviated by distributing computations across network devices. Finally, we analyse the susceptibility of the proposed algorithms to false data injection attacks and consider how such attacks can prevent the scheduling algorithm from converging.

The rest of the paper is structured as follows. In Sect. 2, we present an overview on related work on power consumption scheduling. We proceed in Sect. 3 with a presentation of the system model and formulating our power consumption scheduling algorithm. In Sect. 4, we present the ADMM approach, and then proceed in Sects. 5 and 6 to describe the decentralised and fully decentralised schemes, respectively. In Sect. 7, we show how network unreliability can be exploited to provoke false data injection attacks. Finally, we offer concluding statements in Sect. 8.

## 2  Related Work

Demand Side Management (DSM) facilitates power demand profile smoothing across time by avoiding peak power periods [9]. These solutions minimise the power costs while guaranteeing user satisfaction; this can be achieved through optimisation methods [2,3]. Standard approaches to addressing such optimisation problems on smart grid networks include dual decomposition, and augmented lagrangian methods [10]. However, dual decomposition methods are not robust, requiring many technical conditions, such as strict convexity and finiteness of all local cost functions. Augmented Lagrangian methods can be used to bring robustness to the gradient method, and in particular, to yield convergence without assumptions like strict convexity or finiteness of the objective function [6]. Nevertheless, this method has the disadvantage of not being separable across the devices in the network. ADMM can be used to achieve both separability and robustness for distributed optimisation [6]. Kraning et al. [7] studied an energy management model for a large-scale electrical power network using ADMM. The problem is solved in a distributed manner by alternating between the parallel optimisation of single device objective functions and computing average power imbalances in the nets which the devices belong to. Wei *et al.* [11] proposed an asynchronous ADMM algorithm with a convergence rate of $O(1/k)$, where $k$ is the number of iterations. Although their method applies to a general network utility maximization problem, the results can be adapted to solve the power consumption scheduling problem. This work employs a decentralised optimisation approach based on the ADMM method to solve the power consumption scheduling problem in a distributed manner.

## 3    System Model and Problem Formulation

We describe our MG architecture and formulate the power consumption scheduling problem as a convex optimisation problem. We consider a decentralised MG that consists of a finite set of residential households and small businesses denoted by $H = \{h_1, ..., h_N\}$, where $h_i$ represents the $i^{th}$ household and $1 \leq i \leq N$, and a central controller (utility) that coordinates the operations of the MG. The smart micro-grid (SMG) network combines a power and a communication network, interconnecting households and utility.

**Power Network Model.** The power network model, based on renewable distributed energy resources (DERs) consists of a set of nearby households equipped with renewable generators and/or distributed energy storage and a set of distribution lines that connect household and represents the power line. Let $(H_g \subseteq H)$ denotes the subset of households with generators, $H_s$ denotes the subset of households with small storage, and $H_r$ denotes the subset of users without generators and/or storage devices. The utility generates part of the electricity in the MG and facilitates efficient exchange of energy in the community as well as participating in a short-term wholesale market. The utility provider buys electricity from competing generators in the MG and then retails it to consumers (households).

**Communication Network Model.** Each household $h \in H$ may have a set of electric appliances consuming energy, a distributed generator and a energy storage system. The set of electric appliances in a particular household denoted $\mathcal{A}_h = a_{h,1}, ..., a_{h,A}$ contains four types of loads: resistive load, inductive load, non-linear load and composite load [12] that might be interruptible, uninterruptible and deferrable. Low cost and inaccurate sensors are attached to the appliances to measure consumption and transmit to the local controller (LC) via unreliable communication networks; measurements are likely to be untrustworthy. To address the data inaccuracy issue, we assume that the appliance power consumption is bounded by a minimum and a maximum value representing the lower bound and upper bound. We consider the upper bound value for the scheduling.

The system can be represented by a graph $\mathcal{G} = (\mathcal{V}, \mathcal{E})$, where $\mathcal{V}$ and $\mathcal{E}$ are respectively the set of nodes and the set of edges. Each edge is represented with $\{i, j\} = \{j, i\}$, and $\{i, j\} \in \mathcal{E}$ means that nodes $i$ and $j$ communicate directly and thus can exchange their estimates. The nodes can be a LC (scheduler) at the household (e.g. mobile devices that automatically control the distributed generations (DGs), and loads locally in the households) and the central controller at the utility. At a given interval of time, the LC collects the snapshot of energy consumption [13]. The LC also communicates load demand

and/or generation of the household to which the device is attached. The utility analyses the data considering weather forecast of wind speed and solar radiation. This helps to predict the household load demand as much as possible based on power consumption patterns [14].

We use a continuous discrete-time model with a finite horizon, $\mathcal{T} = \{1, 2, ..., T\}$, where $T$ is finite and divided into $T$ equal intervals of size $\Delta t$. Since our scheduling algorithm operates over an unreliable network, we consider an asynchronous ADMM where information can be lost or delayed during communications. The asynchronous ADMM uses the value from the previous transmission to substitute for missing information due to loss and/or delay. We assume that the total load of a household $h$ at $T$ time slot is denoted as $l_h = (l_h^1, ..., l_h^T)$, and the total load $L_h$ across all households at each time slot $t \in \mathcal{T}$ can be calculated as: $L_t = \sum_{h \in H} l_h^t$

**Appliance Models.** For each appliance $a \in \mathcal{A}_h$, we define $p_{a,h} = (p_{a,h}^1, ..., p_{a,h}^T)$ the power consumption scheduling vector of each appliance $a \in \mathcal{A}_h$ over $\mathcal{T}$, $p_{a,h} \in \mathbb{R}^T$, where $p_{a,h}^t$ the power consumption that is scheduled at time slot $t$ for appliance $a \in \mathcal{A}_h$ in household $h$. The set of energy consumption schedules for all appliances in a household $h \in H$ at time horizon $\mathcal{T}$, is denoted as $P_h$ where $P_h = p_{a,h}, \forall a \in \mathcal{A}_h$ and can be represented with a matrix of dimension $|\mathcal{A}_h| \times T$. The total load of a particular household $h \in H$ denoted $P_h$ is the sum of four types of loads: resistive load, inductive load, nonlinear load and composite load [12]. For load scheduling, each category of appliances is studied according to the level of priority, the interruptibility during operation and the energy consumption. The latter represents consumption patterns over a fixed time interval.

Loads are given priority according to associated power consumption patterns observed between load and operation processes. Loads are classified as either resistive, inductive, and/or composite [12]. In addition to load characterisations, the power consumption behaviour of household devices can be categorised as either interruptible or non-interruptible.

Finally, consumer preferences are accounted for in the scheduling algorithm by allowing consumers to specifying appliance operation preferences [15]. Households and the utility provider jointly determine the energy to be allocated to a household and specify an optimal appliance schedule using the ADMM algorithm. The utility provider sets the prices at a time period and communicates to the households. Upon receiving the price signal, each household solves its own scheduling problem. The solution is based on the short-term ahead scheduling algorithm, where the price of electric energy for next time interval is determined based on short term data forecast. A priority level is allocated to each appliance and the scheduler, schedules the appliances with highest priority level first. If resources are not adequate in that requested time slot a request is denied.

### 3.1   Consumption Scheduling Model

Short term power consumption scheduling in the MG is based on the prior information. Prior information enables the utility to estimate the amount of load demand and renewable power generation of household, e.g. based on weather forecast. However, due to estimation errors and variations in amounts of power generated from renewable sources. It is possible to have deviations between the predetermined power supply and demand. Thus, the utility purchases electricity from household with generation or storage capacity.

Assuming intermittent renewable energy can be predicated using a short-term prediction, the total generation capacity of the set of households $h \in H$ is represented by $G_h$. The household power generation over $T$ time slots is given by $g_h = g_h^t + \epsilon_{g,h}^t, \forall t \in \mathcal{T}$, and it is constrained by $0 \leq g_h^t \leq G_h, \forall t \in \mathcal{T}, \forall h \in H_g$, where $g_h^t$ denotes the distributed generation of the household $h \in H_g$ and $\epsilon_{g,h}^t$ is the prediction error considered with distribution $N(0, \sigma_g^2)$

The power demand projected ($Q_{MG}$) for the power consumption scheduling horizon $\mathcal{T}$ is defined by $Q_{MG}^t = Q_{pg}^t + Q_G^t + Q_s^t$, where $Q_{pg}^t = \sum_{h \in H_g} g_h^t$ is the predicated renewable generation for the set of households $h \in H_g$, $Q_G^t$ is the predicated utility generation and $Q_s^t$ is the energy available on battery at the scheduling horizon.

Let $g_h^t$ be the predicated generation of household $h \in H_g$ at time $t \in \mathcal{T}$. When $g_h^t < l_h^t$, the generation of the household does not covert demand and $h$ purchases electricity from the utility. Otherwise, $g_h^t > l_h^t$, and the household sells back extra generation to the utility. The utility generation at time horizon $\mathcal{T}$ is given by $Q_G^t = \sum_{h \in H_r} l_h^t + \sum_{h \in H_s} l_h^t + \sum_{h \in H_g} \left( l_h^t - g_h^t \right) \forall t \in \mathcal{T}$.

As the generation from both household and utility are different from the conventional power generation, renewable energy generation does not consume fuel sources. For simplicity, we assume a zero generation cost. Thus, the MG available energy $Q_{MG}^t$ cannot be greater than the MG capacity, i.e, $0 \leq Q_{MG}^t \leq Q_G^{max}, \forall t \in \mathcal{T}$

When the utility generation is not enough to meet the demand, utility buys excess generation from a set of households $h \in H_g$. The total cost $C_u(q_h)$ for supply generally consists of the generation cost and the energy purchase cost from the household $h \in H_g$. However as the generation cost is equal to zero, the supplier cost is only the cost of purchasing energy. Let $p^t$ denote the electricity price set by the utility at time $t$, and let $q_h = q_h^t, \forall t \in \mathcal{T}$ denote the amount of power purchased from the household $h$. The total utility cost for electricity $C_u(q_h)$ is given by $C_u(q_h) = \sum_{t=1}^{T} p^t \sum_{h \in H_g} \left( g_h^t - l_h^t \right), \forall g_h^t > l_h^t$.

Since the utility needs to satisfy the power demand, the total cost on the utility end, taking into account user satisfaction cost is given by $C_u = C_u(q_h) + \sum_{t=1}^{T} \sum_{h \in H} s_h^t$

Power consumption scheduling problem at the household level is usually solved by finding the optimal loads scheduling that minimises the household cost, and this in turn flattens the aggregated load curve and reduce the cost to the utility [16]. Let $C_{U,h}$ denotes the total cost function associated to each household $h \in H$. $C_{U,h}$ encompasses the cost related to the use of energy, the satisfaction cost induced by the operating mode mismatch, the cost of operating the battery, and the penalty cost.

A penalty cost function is associated to a duration of an interruption $C(P_{en}^t)$. Similar to the function described in [17], we consider a piecewise linear convex function of the form $C(x) = k_i x + b_i$ to approximate the penalty cost function $C(P_{en}^t)$.

The energy cost (the cost of purchasing energy from the utility) for the household $h \in H$ at time $t \in \mathcal{T}$ is given by $C_{a,h}^t = \sum_{t \in \mathcal{T}} \sum_{a \in \mathcal{A}_h} p^t l_h^t$, where $p^t$ is a dynamic price provided by utility.

Each household chooses a list of appliances and a preferred time for operation. Furthermore, since different households may have diverse preferences, it is not trivial to characterize them with a precise mathematical model. However, according to O'Neill et al. [18] the utility function is an abstract method used to model household preference. Similarly, we follow the same approach in this paper and assume that households would prefer to have their appliances operate sooner than later. This preference can be expressed as a strictly concave utility function that represents satisfaction of the user regarding the schedule. But we rather choose to work with the negation of this function, namely a dissatisfaction function that captures the dissatisfaction of the consumers (due to delaying or advancing the operation of an appliance). We denote $\bar{U}\left(p_{a,h}^{t}\right)$ as dissatisfaction of consumer when running appliance $a \in \mathcal{A}_{\langle}$. Depending on the priority level and the interruptibility, the dissatisfaction function may take different forms [19].

- For interruptible loads, $\bar{U}\left(p_{a,h}\right)$ can be defined as $\bar{U}\left(p_{a,h}\right) = \sum_{t \in \mathcal{T}} \bar{U}\left(p_{a,h}^{t}\right)$
- For deferrable loads such as a composite load, $\bar{U}\left(p_{a,h}\right)$ can be defined as $\bar{U}\left(p_{a,h}\right) = \bar{U}\left(\sum_{t \in \mathcal{T}} p_{a,h}^{t} \varDelta t\right)$

The battery is an energy storage device that flattens the power load by storing energy during low-cost (high-production) periods for use during high-cost periods. We assume that a subset of households $H_{s}$ each have a battery storage device. At each interval, one can either recharge or discharge the battery, but not both at the same time. Each battery has a total capacity $B_{s}^{\max}$, and let $Q_{c,h}^{t}$, $Q_{d,h}^{t}$ and $Q_{s,h}^{t}$ denote the energy charged, discharged and stored at time $t \in \mathcal{T}$ respectively. The charging and discharging power levels at each time $t$ are bounded, and satisfy the following constraints:

$$0 \leq Q_{c,h}^{t} \leq Q_{c,h}^{\max}, \forall t \in \mathcal{T}, \forall h \in H_{s}$$
$$0 \leq Q_{d,h}^{t} \leq Q_{d,h}^{\max}, \forall t \in \mathcal{T}, \forall h \in H_{s},$$

where $Q_{c,h}^{\max}$ and $Q_{d,h}^{\max}$ denote the maximum charging and discharging rates, respectively. The energy stored in the battery should be non-negative and not greater than the battery capacity, and thus satisfies the following constraint $0 \leq Q_{s,h}^{t} \leq B_{s}^{\max}, \forall t \in \mathcal{T}, \forall h \in H_{s}$

The life-time of energy storage is usually characterized by the number of charging/discharging cycles that the battery storage can sustain, and repeated charging and discharging cause ageing of the battery devices. Therefore, let $c_{s}$ denote the unit cost of charging and discharging, and the total cost of operating a battery storage is modelled as follows, $C\left(b_{s}\right) = c_{s}\left(\sum_{t \in \mathcal{T}} Q_{c,h}^{t} + \sum_{t \in \mathcal{T}} Q_{d,h}^{t}\right)$ [20,21], where $b_{s}$ denotes the vector of charging and discharging amount over the scheduling horizon $\mathcal{T}$, respectively. Therefore, the total cost of the household is given as follows:

$$C_{U,h}^{t} = \begin{cases} C(P_{en}^{t}) + \sum_{t \in \mathcal{T}} \sum_{a \in \mathcal{A}_{h}} \bar{U}\left(p_{a,h}\right) + C_{a,h} & \text{if} \quad h \in H_{r} \\ C(P_{en}^{t}) + \sum_{t \in \mathcal{T}} \sum_{a \in \mathcal{A}_{h}} \bar{U}\left(p_{a,h}\right) + C_{a,h} + C\left(b_{s}\right) & \text{if} \quad h \in H_{s} \\ C(P_{en}^{t}) + \sum_{t \in \mathcal{T}} \sum_{a \in \mathcal{A}_{h}} \bar{U}\left(p_{a,h}\right) + C_{h,buy} & \text{if} \quad h \in H_{g} \\ C(P_{en}^{t}) + \sum_{t \in \mathcal{T}} \sum_{a \in \mathcal{A}_{h}} \bar{U}\left(p_{a,h}\right) + C_{h,buy} + C\left(b_{s}\right) & \text{if} \quad h \in H_{g}, h \in H_{s} \end{cases}$$

For a household with generation $h \in H_{g}$, the energy cost also includes the profit they make by selling electricity to the utility. The cost function $C_{h,buy}$ is given by $C_{h,buy} = C_{a,h} - \sum_{t=1}^{T} p^{t}\left(g_{h}^{t} - l_{h}^{t}\right)$.

## 3.2   Optimal Power Consumption Scheduling Problem

Given the data forecast, energy scheduling set, the characteristics of the home electrical appliances and the price model over a time interval. The optimal power consumption scheduling problem (OPCSP) in a micro-grid is a constraint based optimisation problem where the global objective is the sum of objective functions. These functions include consumer and utility actions. Each consumer wishes, to minimise the power consumption by finding the optimal load scheduling solution. Furthermore, the utility, wishes to minimise the cost of operating the MG (power generation and distribution), hence maximize its economic benefit while ensuring that demand and supply are balanced to maintain grid stability. The scheduling problem over a time period is extended to incorporate the cost associated with the usage of appliances such as penalty function due to load interruptions. The OPCSP is formulated as an optimisation problem consisting of a set of variables that minimises the set of objective functions. The optimisation is composed of two types of functions: the local objective function at household $h \in H$, and the global objective function of the total loads of $N$ households at the MG. The local objectives at the household are used to find optimal schedule by minimising the households' cost functions while the utility's objective function is used to minimise its costs (energy purchase) and balance the total power consumption/generation. The power consumption scheduling problem can be formulated as follows:

$$\min_{q_h, p_h} \sum_{t=1}^{T} \left( C_u(q_h(t)) + \sum_{a \in A_h} \sum_{h \in H} C_{U,h}(p_h(t)) \right) \quad (1a)$$

$$S.t. \qquad q_h(t) = p_h(t), \forall_t \in T \quad (1b)$$

$$p_{a,h}(t)^{\min} \le p_{a,h}(t) \le p_{a,h}(t)^{\max}, \forall t \in \mathcal{T}, E_h^{\min} \le \sum_{a \in \mathcal{A}_h} l_h^t \le E_h^{\max}, \forall t \in \mathcal{T} \quad (1c)$$

$$0 \le Q_{c,h}(t) \le Q_{c,h}^{\max}, \forall t \in \mathcal{T}, \forall h \in H_s \quad (1d)$$

$$0 \le Q_{d,h}(t) \le Q_{d,h}^{\max}, \forall t \in \mathcal{T}, \forall h \in H_s, 0 \le Q_{s,h}(t) \le B_s^{\max}, \forall t \in \mathcal{T}, \forall h \in H_s \quad (1e)$$

$$0 \le Q_{MG}^t \le Q_G^{\max}, \forall t \in \mathcal{T}, L_t = \sum_{h \in H} \sum_{a \in \mathcal{A}_h} E_{a,h} \quad (1f)$$

In the above objective function (1a), $C_{U,h}$ denotes the household cost function described in the household cost model, and $C_u$ represents the utility cost function. Constraint (1b) is the power supply-demand balance equation for each time slot $t$, and constraint (1c) is the appliances operational constraints. Constraints (1d)–(1e) are the battery storage operational constraints, and 1f is the MG generation constraint.

The objective function (1a) is considered as convex function, and the minimisation of this problem can lead to an optimal solution. The problem (1a) can be solved at the micro-grid central controller in a centralised way; however, the controller needs the private information about the energy usage/generation from the micro-grid components. Requiring such information raises privacy concerns. Furthermore, the centralised approach causes a significant burden of computation. Alternatively, the solution of (1a) can be obtained efficiently by using distributed convex optimisation algorithms. This work focuses on a distributed optimisation approach based on the ADMM to solve the power consumption scheduling problem distributively after decomposing it into many smaller problems.

## 4   The ADMM Approach

In this section we briefly describe the ADMM which was introduced in the mid-seventies [22], and recently reviewed in [6]. This is an algorithm that solves convex optimisation problems by decomposing them into smaller optimisation problems, each of which are then easier to solve in a distributed manner. The ADMM solves problems of the form:

$$\min_{x_1, x_2} \quad f_1(x_1) + f_2(x_2) \quad \text{subject to} \quad A_1 x_1 + A_2(x_2) = c \tag{2}$$

with variables $x_i \in \mathbb{R}^{n_i}$, where $f_i : \mathbb{R}^{n_i} \to \mathbb{R}$ are closed, proper, convex functions; $A_i \in \mathbb{R}^{m \times n_i}$ are given matrices; and $c \in \mathbb{R}^m$ is a given vector.

*Augmented Lagrangian* methods yield convergence without assumptions like strict convexity or finiteness of $f_i$ [6]. Thus, the augmented Lagrangian for (2) is defined as follows:

$$\mathcal{L}_\rho(x_1, x_2, \lambda) = f_1(x_1) + f_2(x_2) - \lambda^T (A_1 x_1 + A_2 x_2 - c) + \frac{\rho}{2} \|A_1 x_1 + A_2 x_2 - c\|_2^2,$$

where $\lambda \in \mathbb{R}^m$ is the Lagrange multiplier and $\rho > 0$ is the penalty parameter.

First, the augmented Lagrangian is minimized with respect to the first variable $x_1$; next, using the new value for $x_1$, $\mathcal{L}_\rho$ is minimized with respect to $x_2$. Finally, the dual variable $\lambda$ is updated as follows:

$$x_1^{k+1} := \underset{x}{\operatorname{argmin}} \, L_\rho(x_1, x_2^k, \lambda^k)$$

$$x_2^{k+1} := \underset{y}{\operatorname{argmin}} \, L_\rho(x_1^{k+1}, x_2, \lambda^k) \tag{3}$$

$$\lambda^{k+1} := \lambda^k + \rho(A_1 x_1^{k+1} + A_2 x_2^{k+1} - c)$$

Thus, $x_1$ and $x_2$ are updated in an alternating fashion, which accounts for the term *alternating direction*. Separating the minimisation over $x_1$ and $x_2$ is precisely what allows for decomposition when $f_1(x_1)$ or $f_1(x_2)$ are separable, which will be useful in our algorithm's design. The drawback of the standard ADMM method is that it partitions the problem into only two sub-problems and thus cannot be implemented in a distributed way for a larger network. One way is to simply replace the two-block alternating minimisation scheme sequentially (the Gauss-Seidel update fashion), i.e., update $x_i$ for $\{i = 1, 2, ..., N\}$. This approach updates the blocks one after another, which is not suitable for parallelization. To overcome this disadvantage, the Jacobi-type scheme updates all the $N$ blocks in parallel [23]. In the proximal Jacobian Multi-block ADMM, the update of $x_i$ is

$$x_i^{k+1} = \operatorname{argmin} \mathcal{L}_\rho(x_i, \{x_j^k\}_{j \neq i}, \lambda^k) + \frac{1}{2} \|x_i - x_i^k\|_{\mathbf{P_i}}^2 \quad \text{where} \quad \|x_i\|_{\mathbf{P_i}}^2 = x_i^T \mathbf{P_i} x_i \tag{4}$$

for some symmetric and positive semi-definite matrix $\mathbf{P_i} \succeq 0$. When the $x_i-$ sub-problem is not strictly convex, adding the proximal term [24] can make the sub-problem of $x_i$ strictly or strongly convex, and make the problem more stable. The update of Lagrangian multiplier in proximal Jacobian ADMM is $\lambda^{k+1} = \lambda^k - \gamma\rho(\sum_{i=1}^N A_i x_i^{k+1} - c)$, where $\gamma > 0$ is the damping parameter. The resulting optimisation problem is solved with the ADMM, where convergence is guaranteed if the following requirements are satisfied [6]:

1. The functions $f_i$ are closed, proper, and convex
2. The Lagrange function $\mathcal{L}_\rho$ has a saddle point $(x_1^*, x_2^*, \lambda^*) \in \mathcal{R}$ such that
   $\mathcal{L}_\rho(x_1^*, x_2^*, \lambda) \leq \mathcal{L}_\rho(x_1^*, x_2^*, \lambda^*) \leq \mathcal{L}_\rho(x_1, x_2, \lambda^*)$

Wei et al. [23] proved the global convergence of Jacobian ADMM for appropriately chosen regularization matrices $\mathbf{P}_i$. Moreover, they showed that Jacobian ADMM has a convergence rate of $o(1/k)$. In Sects. 5 and 6, we employ the multi-block ADMM to solve the power consumption scheduling problem in a distributed manner. Liu et al. [25] discuss the use of Multi-block ADMM for smart-grid applications.

## 5 Decentralised Optimisation of Power Consumption

In a centralised control approach, all information about the consumers' utility functions can be collected and an efficient energy consumption schedule can be characterized as the solution of optimisation problem (1a). However, the centralised approach requires high computational capabilities at the micro-grid central controller, which is neither efficient nor scalable in resource constrained micro-grid environment. As alternative approach, we study a decentralised power consumption scheduling algorithm using ADMM to solve the optimisation problem (1a). The resulting power consumption scheduling solution is given as Algorithm 1, where each LC $h$ is responsible for updating its own $(p_h^{k+1}, \lambda^{k+1})$ using the most recent $q_h$ value (denoted $\tilde{q}_h$) received from the central controller. Analogous to Eq. (3), the value of $p_h^{k+1}$ and $\lambda_h^{k+1}$ can be updated as follows:

$$p_h(t)^{k+1} = \underset{p_h(t)}{\text{argmin}}\, C_h(p_h(t)^k) + \langle \lambda_h^{k_h}, p_h(t)^k \rangle + \frac{\rho}{2}\|p_h(t)^k - \tilde{q}_h\|^2 \tag{5a}$$

$$\lambda_h^{k+1} = \lambda_h^{k_h} + \rho(p_h(t)^{k+1} - \tilde{q}_h) \tag{5b}$$

We consider $q_h$ as the load which is suggested by the central controller to minimize the fluctuation in the power generation and consumption, and $p_h$ as the load according to the consumers' own benefit. In a synchronization communication model, the central controller must wait for the $p_h^{k_i+1}$ updates from all the $N$ LCs. One draw back in this approach is that the central controller has to wait for all updates $(p_h)$ from all the LC before updating $\lambda$ resulting in the straggler problem[1]. A similar approach is discussed in [26]. We consider an asynchronous algorithm, where instead of a full synchronization on all LCs' reports in each ADMM iteration, a partial synchronization is only required. Updates from the more swift LCs are incorporated more frequently by the central controller, while those from the slower LCs are not allowed to be older than a certain maximum delay. We consider the central controller node keeps a clock $k$, which

---

[1] allows the system to move forward only at the pace of the slowest LC.

is incremented by 1 from zero after each $\lambda^{k+1}$ update. Likewise, each LC also has a clock $k_i$, which is also incremented by 1 from zero after each $\lambda_i$ update. We let, $p_h^{k_i}$ (where $i \in \{1, 2, ...N\}$) be the values of $p_h$ when a LC $i$'s clock is at $k_i$; and $\lambda^k$ be the value of $\lambda(k)$ when the central controller's clock is at $k$.

To alleviate the straggler problem, a *partial barrier* can be employed [27]. The central controller only needs to wait for a minimum of $W$ updates, (where $W \geq 1$ and $W < N$). Reliance on this partial barrier with a small $W$ means updates from slower LCs will be incorporated into computations less frequently than faster controllers. To ensure sufficient "freshness" of all the updates, we enforce a *bounded delay* condition: update from every LC has to be serviced by the central controller at least once every $T$ iterations. $T$ is a user-defined parameter ($T \geq 1$), where updates from each LC $i$ can at most be $T$ clock cycles old (with respect to the central controllers clock). When both the minimum $W$ updates and bounded delay conditions are met, the controlling node will proceed with the $q_h$ update. We let $\Phi^k$ be the set of LCs with ($p_h^{k_i}$) updates that are received by controlling node (at iteration k). When the central controller updates, and sends $q_h^{k+1}$ to the LCs in $\Phi^k$ and its clock $k$ is incremented by 1. Analogous to 3, the controller updates $q_h$ as

$$q_h^{k+1} = \operatorname*{argmin}_{q_h} \sum_{h=1}^{N} \langle -\tilde{\lambda}_h, q_h \rangle + \frac{\rho}{2} \|\tilde{p}_h - q_h\|^2 = \frac{1}{N} \sum_{h=1}^{N} (\tilde{p}_h + \frac{1}{\rho} \tilde{\lambda}_h), \tag{6}$$

where $\tilde{p}_h$ and $\tilde{\lambda}_h$ are the most recent $p_h$ and $\lambda_h$ received from LC by the central controller.

---

**Algorithm 1.** Decentralised Asynchronous ADMM Algorithm

---

1  **Central Controller Procedure:**
2  Initialize: $k = 0, \tilde{p}_h^{k_h+1} = 0 \; \tilde{\lambda}_h = 0,$
       $h = 1, 2, ..., N$
3  $\tilde{p}_h^{k_h+1}$ *being the most recent updates*
4  **repeat**
5     **repeat**
6     |   wait;
7     **until** *receive W LC updates and*
       $max(T_1 T_2, ..., T_N) \leq T$;
8     **for** *LC* $h \in \phi^k$ **do**
9     |   $T_h \leftarrow 1$;
10    |   $p_h \leftarrow$ newly received $p_h$ from local controller $h$;
11    |   $\lambda_h \leftarrow$ newly received $\lambda_h$ from local controller $h$;
12    **end**
13    **for** *LC* $h \notin \phi^k$ **do**
14    |   $T_h \leftarrow T_h + 1$;
15    **end**
16    Update $q_h^{k+1}$ by (6);
17    Send $q_h^{k+1}$ to all LC in $\phi^k$;
18 **until** *termination*;
19 $k \leftarrow k + 1$;
20 **until** termination
21 **output** $q_h^k$
22 **Local Controller Procedure:**
23 Initialize: $\lambda_h^0 = 0, k_h = 0$
24 **repeat**
25    update $p_h^{k_h+1}$ by (5a);
26    send $p_h^{k_h+1}$ to the central controller;
27    **repeat**
28    |   wait;
29    **until** $q_h^{k+1}$' *is received from central controller*;
30    Update $\lambda_h^{k_h+1}$ by (5b) ;
31    $k_h \leftarrow k_h + 1$;
32 **until** *termination*;

---

**Correctness Analysis**

- *Partial correctness:* We claim that the loop invariant always hold at the loop test: $k \leq T$ ($k_h \leq T_h$) and $1 \leq W \leq N$ where $T \geq 1$.
- *Base case:* Assuming the loop invariant holds and the loop test passes. Say in first iteration, k = 1 then $k \leq T$ ($k_h \leq T_h$) is satisfied where $T \geq 1$ (considering that T has a considerable number of cycles). An update will occur in both algorithm fragments.
- *Inductive case:* Assume that the loop invariant holds at the loop test, and also that the loop test passes. New values of $k$, $\tilde{p}_h$ and $\tilde{\lambda}_h$ ($\lambda_h$ and $k_h$) will also hold given $h = 1, 2, ..., N$
- *Termination:* The loop always terminates in the presence of at least one LC update ($1 \geq W \leq N$) and at most T clock cycles when $k = T$ ($k_h = T_h$).

## 6  Fully Decentralised Optimisation of Power Consumption

In Sect. 5 the power consumption scheduling problem is solved in a decentralised way, but as micro-grids will be increasingly interconnected in the future, fully decentralised power consumption scheduling will become an important alternative to the decentralised solutions. In this section, we study a fully distributed algorithm to solve the optimisation problem (1a), where the devices make and coordinate their schedules through local communication with their neighbouring nodes. The key feature of this algorithm is that the computation is localised at the nodal level of the micro-grid network, which does not require any form of central coordination.

The OPCSP (1a) can be reformulated using the ADMM formulation made in Sect. 4 as follows:

$$\min_{\{q_h, p_h\}} \sum_{t=1}^{T} \left( \sum_{n=1}^{N} C_u(q_h(t)) + \sum_{m=1}^{M} C_{U,h}(p_h(t)) \right) \tag{7}$$

Constraint (1b) is the power supply-demand balance equation that ensures the total demand is satisfied by the power generation for each time slot $t$. It couples variables across different DGs and loads. Constraint (1c)–(1f) are local constraints that ensure the loads, batteries and generators do not violate operative limits. Let $\lambda := [\lambda^1, , , \lambda^T]$ denote Lagrange multiplier vector associated with the coupling equality constraint. The augmented Lagrangian for Eq. 7 can be given as follows:

$\mathcal{L}_\rho(q_h, p_h, \lambda) = \sum_{t=1}^{T} \sum_{n=1}^{N} C_u(q_h(t)) + \sum_{t=1}^{T} \sum_{m=1}^{M} C_h(p_h(t)) -$
$\sum_{t=1}^{T} \lambda(t) \left( \sum_{n=1}^{N} C_u(q_h(t)) - \sum_{m=1}^{M} C_h(p_h(t)) \right) + \frac{\rho}{2} \| \sum_{t=1}^{T} \left( \sum_{n=1}^{N} C_u(q_h(t)) - \sum_{m=1}^{M} C_h(p_h(t)) \right) \|_2^2 ,$
where $\lambda$ and $\rho/2$ are the penalty coefficients for the first and second order terms of disagreement.

The OPCSP is solved across the LCs of the DERs and loads. That is, at each step $k$, each LC of DG and load solves the primal problem of ensuring that the local constraints hold, then communicates the generation and consumption schedules to their neighbouring nodes. The update of the LCs can be performed concurrently according to the proximal Jacobian multi-block ADMM. The resulting fully decentralised power consumption scheduling solution is given as Algorithm 2. Initially set $k \leftarrow 0$. The LCs of the DGs and loads set their initial schedules and communicate them to the their neighbour nodes. One of the LCs sets the initial $\lambda(k)$, and broadcasts to its neighbour nodes. Then,

- *The LC of each DG unit solves the following problem (analogous to Eq. 4): OPCSP-LC(DG)*

$$q_h(t)^{k+1} = \operatorname{argmin}_{q_h} C_u(q_h(t)) + \rho/2 \sum_{t=1}^{T} \|q_h(t) - p_h(t)^k - \frac{\lambda^k}{\rho}\|_2^2 + \frac{1}{2}\|q_h(t) - q_h(t)^k\|_{P_1}^2$$

  Once $q_h(t)$ is computed, it is broadcasted to the neighbouring nodes while the utility function is kept private.
- *The LC of each load solves the following problem (analogous to Eq. 4): OPCSP-LC(Load)*

$$p_h(t)^{k+1} = \operatorname{argmin}_{p_h(t)} C_h(p_h)^t + \rho/2 \sum_{t=1}^{T} \|(p_h(t)) - (q_h(t))^k - \frac{\lambda^k}{\rho}\|_2^2 + \frac{1}{2}\|p_h(t) - p_h(t)^k\|_{P_1}^2$$
  Once $p_h(t)$ is computed, it is broadcasted to the neighbouring nodes while the information of cost function is kept private.
- The dual updating step $\lambda$ can be computed by any one of the LCs and broadcasted for all neighbouring nodes. That is, after receiving schedules from the neighbouring LCs of DGs and loads, one of the LCs perform a simple update on the dual variable.

Since the information exchanged between the LCs includes only the control signals and schedules, the privacy of the loads (i.e., customer preferences and constraints) and the DGs (i.e., production costs and constraints) are preserved by the power consumption scheduling devices.

---

**Algorithm 2.** Distributed Power Consumption Scheduling using ADMM

---

1  Initialize: $k \leftarrow 0, \rho > 0, \gamma > 0, \lambda^0 \leftarrow 0$
2  **repeat**
3      *The LC at each DG and each load computes a schedule;*
4      *by solving the corresponding OPCSP-LC;*
5      $q_h(t)^{k+1} = \operatorname*{argmin}\limits_{q_h} C_u(q_h(t)) + \rho/2 \sum_{t=1}^{T} \|q_h(t) - p_h(t)^k - \frac{\lambda^k}{\rho}\|_2^2 + \frac{1}{2}\|q_h(t) - q_h(t)^k\|_{P_1}^2$
6      $p_h(t)^{k+1} =$
       $\operatorname*{argmin}\limits_{p_h(t)} C_h(p_h(t)) + \rho/2 \sum_{t=1}^{T} \|(p_h(t)) - (q_h(t))^k - \frac{\lambda^k}{\rho}\|_2^2 + \frac{1}{2}\|p_h(t) - p_h(t)^k\|_{P_1}^2$
7      *Update $\lambda$ using one of the local controllers in each period;*
8      $\lambda(t)^{k+1} = \lambda(t)^k - \gamma\rho \left( \sum_{n=1}^{N} q_h(t+1) - \sum_{m=1}^{M} p_h(t+1) \right)$
9      $k \leftarrow k + 1;$
10 **until** *convergence;*

---

## 7  Security

Despite its importance, the security of power consumption scheduling algorithms have not received significant attention. The security of the decentralised power consumption scheduling as a whole may depend on the security of the data exchange between the LCs and central controller [28]. The reason for this is that attackers may compromise meter measurements and prevent the decentralised consumption scheduling to converge to the optimal value, or forcing toward a certain values of the attacker's interest. It is thus important to understand the potential vulnerabilities of power consumption scheduling algorithms, i.e., how a compromised data exchange between controllers could affect the power consumption scheduling solutions.

A number of cyberattacks against smart grids have been studied [29,30]. Examples include denial of services attacks, data injection and replay attacks, and timing attacks. Among these attacks, *false data injection* attacks against the state estimation of power grids has been extensively studied due to the serious threat it raises to the operation of the power grid [31–33]. Generally, sensor measurements used for state estimation might be inaccurate due to device misconfigurations, failures, or malicious actions. These inaccuracies can affect state estimations [34]. Many techniques have been proposed to detect, identify and correct bad data measurements, which are based on measurement residuals [35]. However, Liu *et al.* [31] observed that the traditional detection is not able to differentiate between unintentional errors and malicious intrusions attributed to false data injection attacks. They further showed that the attack is required to compromise a number of meters in order to bypass detection, and this type of attack is called *stealth attack* that needs to be launched in a coordinator manner and requires full knowledge of the network configuration.

The security of demand side management programs has been recently explored in [28,36]. For example, Mohsenian-Rad and Leo-Garcia [28] studied attacks against the consumption sector, by investigating load altering attacks and proposed a cost-efficient load protection strategy. Amini *et al.* [36] studied dynamic load altering attacks that attempt to control and change a group of unsecured controllable loads in order to damage the grid through circuit overflow or other mechanisms. There are a variety of load types that are potentially vulnerable to load altering attacks, e.g., controllable loads that automatically respond to price signals and loads in direct load control programs.

Recently, many security attacks against micro-grids have also been reported in [37,38]. In this section, we study the vulnerability of the decentralised power consumption scheduling with respect to false data injection attacks. The reason for this is that the decentralised consumption scheduling algorithm can be prevented from converging to the optimal value, or forced to converge towards values that lend the attacker an advantage.

## 7.1 Attack Model

We assume that the adversary has the capability to manipulate LCs' power consumption measurements, either by compromising the LCs or the communication between the LCs and the central controller. However, the attacker is restricted to compromising the measurements from only specific LCs. Liu *et al.* presented false data injection attacks that can bypass a bad measurement detection algorithm in [31]. Here, we summarize the basic attack principle behind the Liu *et al.* approach.

We assume that there are $q$ meters that provide $m$ measurements $q_1, ..., q_m$, and there are $n$ state variables $p_1, ..., p_n$. The relationship between these $m$ meter measurements and $\mathbf{n}$ state variables can be characterized by an $\mathbf{mn}$ matrix $\mathbf{H}$. The attacker generates malicious measurements based on the matrix $\mathbf{H}$, and then injects the malicious measurements into the compromised meters to undermine the state estimation process. The injected malicious measurements can introduce arbitrary errors into the output of state estimation without being detected by the existing approaches. Let $\mathbf{q_a}$ represent the vector of observed measurements that may contain malicious data. $\mathbf{q_a}$ can be represented as $\mathbf{q_a} = \mathbf{q} + \mathbf{a}$, where $\mathbf{q} = (q_1, ..., q_m)^T$ is the vector of original measurements and $\mathbf{a} = (a_1, ..., a_m)^T$ is the malicious data added to the original measurements. The attacker can choose any non-zero arbitrary vector as the attack vector $\mathbf{a}$, and then construct the malicious measurements $\mathbf{q_a} = \mathbf{q} + \mathbf{a}$. Let $\tilde{\mathbf{p}}_{bad}$ and $\tilde{\mathbf{p}}$ denote the estimates of $\mathbf{p}$ using the malicious measurements $\mathbf{q_a}$ and the original measurements $\mathbf{q}$, respectively. $\tilde{\mathbf{p}}_{bad}$ can be represented as $\tilde{\mathbf{p}} + \mathbf{c}$, where $\mathbf{c}$ is a non-zero vector of length $\mathbf{n}$. Note that $\mathbf{c}$ reflects the estimation error injected by the attacker. The traditional bad measurement detection algorithm computes the $L_2$-norm of the corresponding measurement residual to check whether there exist bad measurements or not. Specifically, $\|\mathbf{q} - \mathbf{H}\tilde{\mathbf{p}}\|$ is compared with a threshold value $\tau$, and the presence of bad measurements is inferred if $\|\mathbf{q} - \mathbf{H}\tilde{\mathbf{p}}\| > \tau\|$, where $\mathbf{q} - \mathbf{H}\tilde{\mathbf{p}}$ (measurement residual) is the difference between the vector of observed measurements and estimated measurements. However, such a detection approach can be bypassed if the attack vector $\mathbf{a}$ is a linear combination of the column vectors of $\mathbf{H}$, $\mathbf{q_a}$ can pass the detection as long as $\mathbf{q}$ can pass the detection. In other words, if the attacker can use $\mathbf{Hc}$ as the attack vector $\mathbf{a}$ (i.e., $\mathbf{a} = \mathbf{Hc}$), then the $L_2$-norm of the measurement residual of $\mathbf{q_a}$ is equal to that of $\mathbf{q}$. The feasibility of the stealth false data injection attack can be described as follows [31]:

$$\|\mathbf{q_a} - \mathbf{H}\tilde{\mathbf{p}}_{bad}\| = \|\mathbf{q} + \mathbf{a} - \mathbf{H}(\tilde{\mathbf{p}} + \mathbf{c})\| = \|\mathbf{q} + \mathbf{a} - \mathbf{H}\tilde{\mathbf{p}} - \mathbf{Hc}\| = \|\mathbf{q} - \mathbf{H}\tilde{\mathbf{p}} + (\mathbf{a} - \mathbf{Hc})\| = \|\mathbf{q} - \mathbf{H}\tilde{\mathbf{p}}\|$$

where $\mathbf{a} = \mathbf{Hc}$. It is also reported that if the attacker can compromise $k$ specific meters, the attack vector always exists [31]. This attack principle will be used to analyse the vulnerability of the decentralised power consumption scheduling algorithm with respect to false data injection in Sect. 7.2.

## 7.2 ADMM with False Data Injection Attacks

This section presents a vulnerability analysis of the decentralised algorithm with respect to false data injection attacks, and describes how an attacker that has successfully compromised a set of devices can manipulate the power profile exchanged between the LCs and the central controller. We summarise the decentralised power consumption scheduling algorithm in Sect. 5 as follows:

Consider the $k^{th}$ iteration.

- Step 1: The central controller sets the $q_h^k$, and sends to the LCs
- Step 2: Using the control signal from the central controller, the LCs calculate the dual-primal update $(p_h^{k+1}, \lambda_h^k)$, and communicate the value to the central controller

$$p_h(t)^{k+1} = \text{argmin}_{p_h(t)} C_h(p_h(t)^k) + \langle \lambda_h^{k_h}, p_h(t)^k \rangle + \frac{\rho}{2}\|p_h(t)^k - \tilde{q}_h\|^2$$

$$\lambda_h^{k+1} = \lambda_h^{k_h} + \rho(p_h(t)^{k_h+1} - \tilde{q}_h)$$

- Step 3: The central controller updates $q_h^{k+1}$, and sends back to the LCs for their next update

$$q_h^{k+1} = \text{argmin}_q h \sum_{h=1}^{N} \langle -\tilde{\lambda}_h, q_h \rangle + \frac{\rho}{2}\|\tilde{p}_h - q_h\|^2 = \frac{1}{N}\sum_{h=1}^{N}(\tilde{p}_h + \frac{1}{\rho}\tilde{\lambda}_h),$$

- Step 4: Test for convergence, $\|\Delta q_h^k\|_2 < \epsilon$
- Step 5: If not, update $k \leftarrow k + 1$, and go to step 2. Else, stop.

The algorithm converges when the maximum update of the coordination signals is smaller than the convergence threshold $\epsilon > 0, \|\Delta q_h{}^k\| < \epsilon$. Once the algorithm converges, a bad data detection algorithm analyses the measurement residual vector to detect and identify faulty measurement data. However, the measurements can be manipulated to ensure that the algorithm does not detect the manipulation [31]. An attacker can compromise part of the LCs or the communication network so that he/she can manipulate the power profile exchanged with the central controller; this value is used as an input to the ADMM algorithm.

The attack vector at iteration $k$ is represented as $\mathbf{a}^k$, or $\ddot{P}_h(t)^k = \tilde{p}_h(t)^k + \mathbf{a}^k$, where $\ddot{P}_h(t)^k$ is the corrupted vector power consumption variable. The vector $\ddot{P}_h(t)$ is used as input to the next iteration$(k + 1)$ of the ADMM at the central controller, instead of the originally vector $\tilde{p}_h(t)$. When the power consumption profile is changed by the manipulation, the control signal will change from $\mathbf{q_h}$ to $\ddot{\mathbf{q}}_{\mathbf{h}}$. It can be calculated by replacing $\tilde{p}_h(t)^k$ to $(\tilde{p}_h(t)^k + \mathbf{a}^k)$ in *step 3*, that is

$\ddot{q}_h{}^{k+1} = \frac{1}{N} \sum_{h=1}^{N} (\tilde{p}_h(t)^k + \mathbf{a}^k + \frac{1}{\rho}\tilde{\lambda}_h)$

In other words, if $\mathbf{a} \neq 0$ then the attack will be able to drive the consensus variable $(q_h)$ by $\mathbf{a}$ to an erroneous solution$(\ddot{\mathbf{q}}_{\mathbf{h}})$ using *step 3* of the ADMM. The attack can prevent the convergence of the algorithm to the optimal value, or drive toward a certain solution of the attacker's interest. If the total demand is lower than the available power, a part of the available power will be wasted and there will be a loss in terms of revenue. On the other hand, if the demand surpasses the available power, serious problems such as black-outs may occur on the users end. An attack on the control signals can be described similarly. A small attack size implies smaller corruption added to the exchanged values, which could make the detection harder. The size of the attack is defined as the Euclidean norm of the attack vector, i.e., $\|\Delta \ddot{\mathbf{P}}_{\mathbf{h}}(\mathbf{t})\|_2$. Thus, it would be natural for the attacker to look for the smallest attack vector that prevents the ADMM from converging. Sandberg *et al.* [39] introduced the notion of a *security index* $\alpha_k$ to characterize the minimum effort needed for a targeted attacks. The security index not only quantifies the minimum effort needed for stealth false data attacks but also characterizes the robustness of the grid against such attacks.

# 8   Conclusions

This paper has studied decentralised DSM for the optimal operation of micro-grids, and addressed the vulnerability of power consumption scheduling algorithms with respect to false data injection attacks. Specifically, we formulated the power consumption scheduling problem as a convex optimisation problem and employed the ADMM to solve the optimisation problem as two decentralised algorithms by distributing computations across every device in the microgird network. In the first case, the central controller sets the control signals to coordinate the consumers' power consumption schedule decisions, and in the second case, the consumers make and coordinate their power consumption schedule decisions through local communications with their direct neighbours in the micro-grid network. The objective of the algorithms is to shift the power consumption of loads to match generation while minimising the electricity cost and consumer dissatisfaction associated with changes in consumption. Such algorithms can also be a desirable alternative to the centralised energy management approaches, especially when highly intermittent renewable energy generation and various load demands pose challenges to the energy management in the micro-grid. We also investigated the vulnerability of the decentralised algorithms with respect to false data injection attacks in the micro-grid environment. Our analysis indicates that false data injection attacks can force the decentralised algorithms into erroneous values or prevent them from converging to optimal values by withholding the delivery of a set of particular measurements.

As future work, we will evaluate the proposed algorithms through numerical simulations.

**Acknowledgments.** This work was partially supported by the joint SANCOOP Programme of the Research Council (NRC) of Norway and the National Research Foundation of South Africa (NRF) under the NRF grant 237817. The authors gratefully thank the anonymous referees for their review comments that helped improve the presentation of the paper.

# References

1. Hatziargyriou, N., Jenkins, N., Strbac, G., Lopes, J.P., Ruela, J., Engler, A., Oyarzabal, J., Kariniotakis, G., Amorim, A.: Microgrids-large scale integration of microgeneration to low voltage grids. CIGRE C6–309, pp. 1–8 (2006)
2. Koutsopoulos, I., Tassiulas, L.: Optimal control policies for power demand scheduling in the smart grid. IEEE J. Sel. Areas Commun. **30**(6), 1049–1060 (2012)
3. Vardakas, J., Zorba, N., Verikoukis, C.: A survey on demand response programs in smart grids: Pricing methods and optimization algorithms. IEEE Commun. Surv. Tutorials **17**(1), 152–178 (2015). First quarter
4. Shi, W., Xie, X., Chu, C.C., Gadh, R.: Distributed optimal energy management in microgrids. IEEE Trans. Smart Grid **6**(3), 1137–1146 (2015)
5. Shi, W., Li, N., Chu, C.C., Gadh, R.: Real-time energy management in microgrids. IEEE Trans. Smart Grid **PP**(99), 1–11 (2015)
6. Boyd, S., Parikh, N., Chu, E., Peleato, B., Eckstein, J.: Distributed optimization and statistical learning via the alternating direction method of multipliers. Found. Trends Mach. Learn. **3**(1), 1–122 (2011)
7. Kraning, M., Chu, E., Lavaei, J., Boyd, S.: Message passing for dynamic network energy management. arXiv preprint arXiv:1204.1106, pp. 1–30, April 2012
8. Kekatos, V., Giannakis, G.: Distributed robust power system state estimation. IEEE Trans. Power Syst. **28**(2), 1617–1626 (2013)
9. Gellings, C., Chamberlin, J.: Demand-side management: Concepts and methods, 2nd edn. PennWell Corporation (1993)
10. Zhang, Y., Gatsis, N., Giannakis, G., Zhang, Y., Gatsis, N., Giannakis, G.B.: Robust energy management for microgrids with high-penetration renewables. IEEE Trans. Sustain. Energy **4**(4), 944–953 (2013)
11. Wei, E., Ozdaglar, A.: On the O(1/k) convergence of asynchronous distributed alternating direction method of multipliers. ArXiv e-prints, July 2013
12. Ambassa, P.L., Wolthusen, S.D., Kayem, A.V., Meinel, C.: Robust snapshot algorithm for power consumption monitoring in computationally constrained micro-grids. In: 2015 IEEE Innovative Smart Grid Technologies - Asia (ISGT ASIA), pp. 1–6, November 2015

13. Ambassa, P.L., Kayem, A.V.D.M., Wolthusen, S.D., Meinel, C.: Secure and reliable power consumption monitoring in untrustworthy micro-grids. In: Doss, R., Piramuthu, S., Zhou, W. (eds.) FNSS 2015. CCIS, vol. 523, pp. 166–180. Springer, Cham (2015). doi:10.1007/978-3-319-19210-9_12

14. Weldehawaryat, G., Wolthusen, S.: Secure distributed demand projection in micro-grids. In: Global Information Infrastructure and Networking Symposium (GIIS), pp. 1–6, October 2015

15. Sou, K.C., Kordel, M., Wu, J., Sandberg, H., Johansson, K.: Energy and CO2 efficient scheduling of smart home appliances. In: 2013 European Control Conference (ECC), pp. 4051–4058, July 2013

16. Yang, P., Chavali, P., Gilboa, E., Nehorai, A.: Parallel load schedule optimization with renewable distributed generators in smart grids. IEEE Trans. Smart Grid 4(3), 1431–1441 (2013)

17. Koutsopoulos, I., Tassiulas, L.: Control and optimization meet the smart power grid: Scheduling of power demands for optimal energy management. In: Proceedings of the 2nd International Conference on Energy-Efficient Computing and Networking. e-Energy 2011, pp. 41–50. ACM, New York (2011)

18. O'Neill, D., Levorato, M., Goldsmith, A., Mitra, U.: Residential demand response using reinforcement learning. In: 2010 First IEEE International Conference on Smart Grid Communications (SmartGridComm), pp. 409–414, October 2010

19. Li, N., Chen, L., Low, S.: Optimal demand response based on utility maximization in power networks. In: 2011 IEEE Power and Energy Society General Meeting, pp. 1–8, July 2011

20. Urgaonkar, R., Urgaonkar, B., Neely, M.J., Sivasubramaniam, A.: Optimal power cost management using stored energy in data centers. In: Proceedings of the ACM SIGMETRICS Joint International Conference on Measurement and Modeling of Computer Systems, SIGMETRICS 2011, pp. 221–232. ACM, New York (2011)

21. Wang, H., Huang, J.: Bargaining-based energy trading market for interconnected microgrids. In: 2015 IEEE International Conference on Communications (ICC), pp. 776–781, June 2015

22. Gabay, D., Mercier, B.: A dual algorithm for the solution of nonlinear variational problems via finite element approximation. Comput. Math. Appl. 2(1), 17–40 (1976)

23. Deng, W., Lai, M.J., Peng, Z., Yin, W.: Parallel multi-block ADMM with o(1/k) convergence. J. Sci. Comput. 71, 1–25 (2016)

24. Parikh, N., Boyd, S.: Proximal algorithms. Found. Trends Optim. 1(3), 127–239 (2014)

25. Liu, L., Han, Z.: Multi-block ADMM for big data optimization in smart grid. In: 2015 International Conference on Computing, Networking and Communications (ICNC), pp. 556–561, February 2015

26. Zhang, R., Kwok, J.: Asynchronous distributed ADMM for consensus optimization. In: Proceedings of the 31st International Conference on Machine Learning (ICML-14), pp. 1701–1709 (2014)

27. Albrecht, J.R., Tuttle, C., Snoeren, A.C., Vahdat, A.: Loose synchronization for large-scale networked systems. In: USENIX Annual Technical Conference, General Track, pp. 301–314 (2006)

28. Mohsenian-Rad, A.H., Leon-Garcia, A.: Distributed internet-based load altering attacks against smart power grids. IEEE Trans. Smart Grid 2(4), 667–674 (2011)

29. Li, X., Liang, X., Lu, R., Shen, X., Lin, X., Zhu, H.: Securing smart grid: cyber attacks, countermeasures, and challenges. IEEE Commun. Mag. 50(8), 38–45 (2012)

30. Wang, W., Lu, Z.: Cyber security in the smart grid: Survey and challenges. Comput. Netw. 57(5), 1344–1371 (2013)

31. Liu, Y., Ning, P., Reiter, M.K.: False data injection attacks against state estimation in electric power grids. In: Proceedings of the 16th ACM Conference on Computer and Communications Security, pp. 21–32. ACM, New York (2009)

32. Feng, Y., Foglietta, C., Baiocco, A., Panzieri, S., Wolthusen, S.D.: Malicious false data injection in hierarchical electric power grid state estimation systems. In: Proceedings of the Fourth International Conference on Future Energy Systems. e-Energy 2013, pp. 183–192. ACM, New York (2013)

33. Vuković, O., Dán, G.: On the security of distributed power system state estimation under targeted attacks. In: Proceedings of the 28th Annual ACM Symposium on Applied Computing, SAC 2013, pp. 666–672. ACM, New York (2013)

34. Bobba, R.B., Rogers, K.M., Wang, Q., Khurana, H., Nahrstedt, K., Overbye, T.J.: Detecting false data injection attacks on DCstate estimation. In: Preprints of the First Workshop on Secure Control Systems, CPSWEEK. vol. 2010 (2010)

35. Monticelli, A.: Electric power system state estimation. Proc. IEEE **88**(2), 262–282 (2000)

36. Amini, S., Mohsenian-Rad, H., Pasqualetti, F.: Dynamic load altering attacks in smart grid. In: 2015 IEEE Power Energy Society Innovative Smart Grid Technologies Conference (ISGT), pp. 1–5, February 2015

37. Mantooth, H.A., Liu, Y., Farnell, C., Zhang, F., Li, Q., Di, J.: Securing DC and hybrid microgrids. In: 2015 IEEE First International Conference on DC Microgrids (ICDCM), pp. 285–286, June 2015

38. Talebi, M., Li, C., Qu, Z.: Enhanced protection against false data injection by dynamically changing information structure of microgrids. In: IEEE 7th Sensor Array and Multichannel Signal Processing Workshop (SAM), pp. 393–396, June 2012

39. Sandberg, H., Teixeira, A., Johansson, K.H.: On security indices for state estimators in power networks. In: 2010 First Workshop on Secure Control Systems (SCS), Stockholm, pp. 1–6 (2010)

# Security Issues and Mitigation
# in Ethernet POWERLINK

Jonathan Yung[1,2(✉)], Hervé Debar[1], and Louis Granboulan[2]

[1] Telecom SudParis, 9 rue Charles Fourier, 91011 Evry, France
Jonathan.yung@telecom-sudparis.eu
[2] Airbus Group Innovations, 12 rue Pasteur, 92152 Suresnes, France

**Abstract.** Ethernet POWERLINK is an industrial Ethernet protocol created for applications with high degree of determinism, and amongst the closest to real-time (class 3 industrial Ethernet protocol). Consequently, it was developed for efficiency and short cycle times, with no security as it would only slow down the communications. In this paper, we show that most of the common known industrial Ethernet attacks cannot be carried out for Ethernet POWERLINK due to its isochronous real-time characteristics. We also show that it is still possible to perform attacks to affect such a system. We thus present five different attacks: a denial of service, a command insertion for a slave and then for a master, and impersonation of a slave and, finally, of a master. These attacks are afterwards validated on a testbed. We finally present proposals to defend against them without adding any major delay in the cyclic communications, by modifying transitions of the state machines of the protocol.

## 1 Introduction

Industrial Ethernet protocols are the evolution of the Fieldbus protocols, which have been adapted to be able to work on Ethernet. This development makes communications easier with standard IT networks, but also simplifies access for an attacker.

Neumann [1] and Jasperneite et al. [2] classify industrial Ethernet in three classes. Class 1 (soft real-time, e.g. MODBUS/TCP, EtherNet/IP) uses the TCP/IP suite to transport and schedule data. Class 2 (hard real-time, e.g. PROFINET RT) directly relies on a standard Ethernet frame; it is faster than the class 1 but, due to the CSMA/CD mechanism, it does not offer real determinism. Finally, class 3 (isochronous real-time, e.g. Ethernet POWERLINK, PROFINET IRT, EtherCAT) also use Ethernet, but with a different technique for medium access control.

Many papers have already discussed attacks and mitigation for class 1 and class 2 protocols. However, there is no work yet on this topic for the class 3.

In this paper, we present several attacks and propose modifications to the Ethernet POWERLINK protocol to defend against them.

The paper is organized as follows: Sect. 2 gives a short overview of Ethernet POWERLINK. In Sect. 3, we present the related work on class 1 and 2 protocols,

N. Cuppens-Boulahia et al. (Eds.): CyberICPS 2016, LNCS 10166, pp. 87–102, 2017.
DOI: 10.1007/978-3-319-61437-3_6

and we analyze its applicability to the Ethernet POWERLINK protocol. Then we present the theory of our attacks in Sect. 4, and how we implemented them in Sect. 5. An adaptation of the protocol to protect against these attacks is showed in Sect. 6.

## 2    Ethernet POWERLINK Protocol

Ethernet POWERLINK [3] is a class 3 industrial Ethernet protocol, specified by the EPSG (Ethernet POWERLINK Standardization Group). It uses the Master/Slave model to achieve deterministic communications: an Ethernet POWERLINK network is composed of one master, called MN (Managing Node, e.g., a PLC) and up to 240 slaves, or CN (Controlled Node, e.g., a sensor or an actuator). A CN can send a message only if it is asked to by the MN, which guarantees that no collisions can occur in proper functioning. It works on top of Ethernet, and the CANopen [4] protocol is used as its application layer to model the network, its configurations and data layout through an object dictionary.

### 2.1    Cycle

Communications in Ethernet POWERLINK are managed by the MN in cycles, divided in two main periods: isochronous and asynchronous. The former is used to exchange critical real-time data through a producer-consumer relationship, when the latter offers the possibility to do normal communications (e.g., non critical commands, legacy Ethernet frame, access to the object dictionary). Only one message can be sent during the asynchronous period, and the sender is designated by the MN. At the end of a cycle, an idle period is added to guarantee constant cycle duration and to minimize jitter. Figure 1 shows the order of all the frames.

**SoC.** The SoC (Start of Cycle) frame is sent by the MN to every CN on the network. It is used to determine the start of a cycle but also to synchronize the clocks of the nodes.

**PReq/PRes.** After the cycle starts, the MN polls data from every CN consecutively. It sends a PReq (Poll Request) frame in unicast to the first CN, which can contain real-time data from the MN. The CN then answers to the MN and to

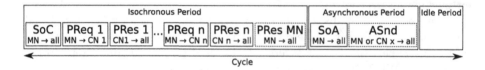

**Fig. 1.** An Ethernet POWERLINK cycle

every other CN with its data, through a PRes (Poll Response) multicast frame. If a CN is interested by this message, it can consume it (slave to slave communications). This frame is also used by a CN to notify the MN that it has one or more messages to send during the asynchronous period, with a priority indication. A timer is set by the MN after having sent the PReq. When this timer expires, the MN sends the PReq to the next CN, even if it did not receive the expected reply from the previous one. When every CN has been contacted, the MN can optionally send additional real-time data to every CN on the network, with a PRes.

**SoA.** The SoA (Start of Asynchronous) frame is used to start the asynchronous period. It is sent by the MN to every CN, and it indicates which device (including the MN) can use the asynchronous period, and what type of frame it can send. If the MN does not have any messages to schedule during this period, it sends a void SoA and the idle period starts.

**ASnd.** The device which has been chosen by the SoA (if any) sends an ASnd (Asynchronous Send) frame to every node. After the ASnd is received or sent by the MN, the idle period starts. When the cycle ends (that is, after a pre-defined time after the last SoC), a new one starts.

## 2.2   Network Management

The NMT (Network Management) defines state machines for the MN and CNs, which describes the different states a device can have from the moment it is started. The MN can change a device state through an ASnd frame called *NMT commands*. Besides, a CN can also ask the MN to send *NMT commands* to another device. Figure 2 presents the state machines of an EPL-mode MN (that is, an MN configured to communicate over Ethernet POWERLINK) and of a CN.

**MN.** When the MN starts, and after basic initialization, verifies that there is not already an MN active on the network, in which case it must stop. If not, it then checks that all the CNs which are defined as mandatory in its application are present with the *ident* and *status* ASnd frame, eventually configures them with the *SDO* ASnd frame and, if a full cycle can be completed without errors, enters the *operational* state. If the communications with one CN are lost, it will check again the CNs. The MN can also be reset with an *NMT command* ASnd frame.

**CN.** When a CN starts, it waits for an SoA or SoC frame. After having received another SoC, it can answer the MN with ASnd frames. The MN is then able to configure it and change its NMT state. In particular, a CN can be stopped with an *NMT command*, until the MN starts it again.

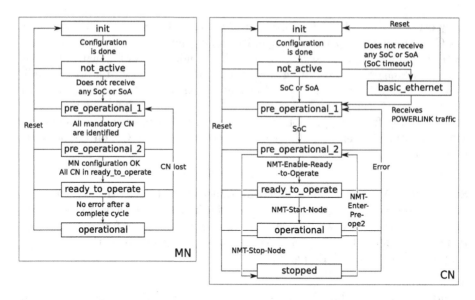

**Fig. 2.** State machine of an EPL-mode MN (left) and of a CN (right)

## 2.3 Threat Model

The architecture we consider in this paper is a PLC (MN) and a few I/O modules connected to the Ethernet POWERLINK network (also called control network) by bus controllers. The PLC can also be connected to another network (process network) on standard Ethernet which can be connected to other PLCs or HMIs or programming stations or to the IT network.

The attacks we present are directly related to the Ethernet POWERLINK protocol: we must therefore access the control network. There are then two possibilities to meet this requirement: starting directly from the control network, or connecting to it through the PLC, by the process network.

In the first case, an attacker can compromise a field device or connect additional equipment on the network. The latter is the easiest, as many Ethernet POWERLINK CNs include an internal hub with at least two ports, on which an attacker can plug a device using a standard Ethernet cable. However it is not possible to disconnect a mandatory CN from the network to replace it by another without restarting the whole network.

In the second case, one would have to compromise the PLC through its legacy Ethernet interface, which is accessible from the process network. Even in the case that these networks cannot be reached from Internet, attacks like Stuxnet [5] which was first spread by an USB stick show that one can still access them. Spenneberg et al. [6] also presents a malware designed specifically for a PLC.

Because an Ethernet POWERLINK network is based on hubs, we do not consider a man-in-the-middle attack, as we will see in the next section.

# 3   Related Work

Many papers present attacks and means of defense for class one and two protocols. However, there is no research for class 3 protocol yet. In this section, we look at those papers to see if the results proposed in the literature can be applied to the Ethernet POWERLINK protocol. We classify the different attacks we have found in four categories, in a similar way as [7]. *Eavesdropping* involves an attacker gaining understanding of the process and of the network by listening the communications on the network. *Interruption* entails that the communications between two devices or in the whole network has been tampered with, either by the suppression of one or several messages, or by the insertion of a substantial traffic to flood and prevent normal communications. *Modification* implies that the attacker intercepted a message sent by an actual device on the network, modified it, and sent it back (man-in-the-middle attack). Finally, *insertion* means that an attacker creates a message and send it on the network.

Eavesdropping in industrial Ethernet is easy as it does not use encryption whatsoever. Huitsing et al. [7] present several attacks of this type against MODBUS/TCP, as well as Bristow [8] which made use of the exception model of this protocol to develop a scanning software to analyze the function codes and the memory of a device. On Ethernet POWERLINK, listening to the network enables passive reconnaissance and mapping of the different CNs, the order of the PReq/PRes exchanges, etc.

Huitsing et al. [7] and Queiroz [9] present interruption attacks on the MODBUS/TCP protocol, but using attack on the TCP protocol. Consequently, these attacks work for all class 1 protocols on TCP, but they are not intended for class 2 or 3 protocols. However, class 3 protocols were designed to have their communications as close to real time as possible, by implementing their own medium access control mechanism. This works perfectly as long as every device on the network is behaving as expected. Class 3 protocols are therefore especially vulnerable to interruption attack. We specify in this paper a way to perform this type of attack on the Ethernet POWERLINK protocol.

Antonioli and Tippenhauer [10] and Åkerberg and Björkman [11] present modification attacks for EtherNet/IP and PROFINET IO respectively, by using ARP cache poisoning. Those attacks however work for switched Ethernet, and the Ethernet POWERLINK specification indicates to only use repeaters.

Paul et al. [12] propose to do a modification attack on PROFINET IO by using DCP, a protocol from the PROFINET suite doing basic device configuration. However, with the Ethernet POWERLINK protocol, if the MN sees two CNs with the same node number, it stops the start-up sequence, which makes this attack impossible in practice.

Finally, the most common type of attack found in the literature is insertion. There are two kind of messages an attacker might want to insert: process data (input or output) and command. Huitsing et al. [7] and Åkerberg and Björkman [11] insert process data messages for respectively MODBUS/TCP and PROFINET. However, this type of message is sent regularly by the devices and the insertion should be repeated regularly to be efficient. In [11] the attack is performed at every cycle, and the message is inserted just before the correct message. As only one message is accepted by PROFINET IO cycle, the correct message is dropped. The Ethernet POWERLINK network is however too prone to collisions in the isochronous period to be able to do this type of attack. In the work of Bhatia et al. [13], an attacker floods the network with process data messages to ensure that its modifications are not overwritten by normal traffic. This is of course totally impossible in an Ethernet POWERLINK network without causing collisions. Finally, Huitsing et al. [7] and Digital Bond [14] present the insertion of commands to modify or stop devices on a MODBUS/TCP and EtherNet/IP network respectively. We show in Sect. 4 that this type of attack is possible on an Ethernet POWERLINK network under certain conditions.

Many authors have been working on securing industrial Ethernet protocols. We classify their articles in three categories. The first category implements a wrapper protocol in the device. The second category adds an intermediary unit between the device and the network (a BITW module, for Bump-In-The-Wire), The third category modifies the protocol to add cryptography services to provide authentication, integrity and/or confidentiality.

The first category focuses principally on securing the TCP and IP layers. Patel [15] studies the use of TLS and IPSec for MODBUS/TCP and DNP3. This approach can only be used for class 1 protocols, with a drastic decrease in performance. It can therefore not be used for Ethernet POWERLINK, which uses neither TCP nor IP.

The second category concerns BITW module. The most well-known solution for industrial Ethernet and more generally ICS (Industrial Control Systems) protocols is AGA-12 [16], which was however withdrawn before completion because of its cost. West [17] shows how one could use it to secure a MODBUS or DNP3 network. Tsang and Smith [18] present another BITW solution adapted from AGA-12. These solutions however imply communication delays that could not fit class 3 protocols for which cycle duration is extremely short. It would besides add a jitter we do not want on a determinist network.

The third category is based on cryptographic techniques. Shahzad et al. [19] and Fovino et al. [20] present a solution for MODBUS/TCP based on RSA signature, with the associated drawback of the slowness of an asymmetric cryptography solution. Hayes and El-Khatib [21] consequently propose to use an HMAC instead. They also use SCTP instead of TCP for MODBUS/TCP to increase availability. Wang and Chu [22] classify the communications of an ICS protocol in four categories: data acquisition, firmware download, control functions and broadcast. It proposes a framework applicable to every protocol (SSCada) based on encryption and MAC. Åkerberg and Björkman [11] also suggest using MAC to protect PROFINET IO communications. Czybik et al. [23] compare different MAC solutions for ICS. The HMAC is on average the most efficient one, and has a calculation time of 50 µs for a 50 or less bytes long frame. For Ethernet POWERLINK, at each cycle, for each CN, the calculation needs to be done for the PReq and the PRes. This adds at least 100 µs latency by CN, which is an important delay for a class 3 protocol. Finally, Patel [15] and the DNP3-SA protocol [24] propose a challenge/response mechanism, which is also impossible for

Ethernet POWERLINK isochronous messages. However, these last two points can be analyzed and possibly reused for the asynchronous period.

## 4 Attacks

We present here a few attacks that are possible on an Ethernet POWERLINK network. Figure 3 summarizes the different steps of all the attacks.

**Denial of Service.** In an Ethernet POWERLINK network, medium access is managed by the Master/Slave model: collisions are avoided because the MN makes sure that there is only one message on the wire in a determined period of time. It is consequently particularly vulnerable to Denial of Service attacks. One can for example flood the network with SoC messages. The MN will then restart due to too many errors, and will stay in the *not_active* state as long as it receives SoC frames.

**ASnd Message Insertion.** During the asynchronous period, only one ASnd frame can be sent, which sender and type is decided by the SoA frame. However, the MN does not check the number of ASnd sent in one cycle, nor if it is coherent with the SoA. The time dedicated to the asynchronous period is set during the MN programming, and depends on the length of the frame one want to send during this phase. Therefore, if no ASnd frame is sent, or if it is short enough, it is possible to insert ASnd messages at that time without any error being logged. There are two main things one can do during this period: NMT commands and object dictionary modifications.

The NMT commands can change the CN NMT state: one can reset the CN configuration, communications, or the application, put it to pre-configured states or stop it. In this last case, the CN will not be able to communicate until it is reset or put back to *pre_operational_1* state.

The object dictionary contains all the configuration of a device, including communication parameters, process data formatting, device profile and manufacturer specific setup, etc. If an item is accessible in *read/write* or in *write only*, it can be modified by every device on the network by a SDO ASnd frame. One interesting example is the errors configurations objects, which defines how you should count the number of errors and the threshold before the CN state changes to *pre_operational_1*. Modifying it would change the way a CN reacts after detecting an error, and could reduce the probability for a next attack to be noticed.

**CN Impersonation.** The previous attack enables stopping a CN with an NMT stop command. The order is immediate, and the targeted CN will stop answering the MN in the next cycle. It is then possible to usurp its communications slots, and to act like the CN, without triggering any errors on the network.

When a CN is stopped, it cannot go back to the *operational* state directly, but must enter in the *pre_operational_1* state. Consequently, if the attacker releases the CN, the MN must also pass through in the *pre_operational_1* state with a "CN lost" error.

**MN Reset.** A CN is not able to send an *NMT command* ASnd frame during the asynchronous period; however, it can ask the MN to do it in its place during the PRes/PReq exchange. When invited, the CN will then send an *NMT request* ASnd frame specifying the recipient and the type of the NMT command it wants. Consequently, the attacker first needs to impersonate a CN and to send a PRes during the isochronous period, with a request to send an ASnd with maximum priority. It can then send an *NMT request* ASnd frame to the MN which will do the actual NMT Command on the next cycle. This method has the advantage over the first attack (denial of service) that it does not create any errors on the MN side.

**MN Impersonation.** When the MN has been reset, either by the denial of service attack or the MN reset attack, it is possible to immediately take its place and exchange data with the CNs. During its start-up phase, the normal MN will then see that there is already an MN on the network and will stay in the *not_active* state, without the opportunity to send any data on the Ethernet POWERLINK network. An error will however be triggered in the MN application, but it will not be able to spread if the MN is not connected to another network (for instance an HMI on a legacy Ethernet interface).

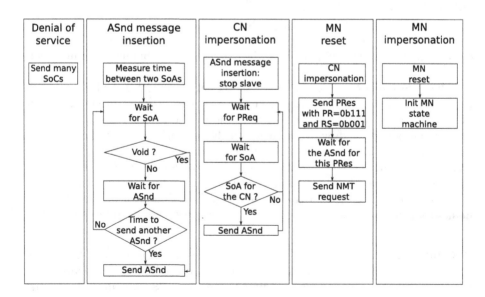

**Fig. 3.** The different steps of the attacks

# 5   Implementation of the Attacks

## 5.1   Testbed

These attacks have been implemented on a testbed, with the hypothesis of a control system where we can plug another device (in our case, a computer). We developed a software to listen for Ethernet POWERLINK communications on the network, collect the information about the MN and all the CNs (node number, identity data, last payload, time between two SoC, etc.), and let an user to launch the different attacks. In particular, it includes a small implementation of a CN and of an MN to do the impersonation attacks.

Two different testbeds have been used to validate the attacks.

The first is the closer to reality in both material and timing constraint and tested the denial of service and the ASnd message insertion. It is composed of a CPU (X20CP1585) connected to a digital output (X20DO9322) and a digital input (X20DI9371) through a bus controller (X20BC0083), all from the B&R's X20 system[1]. However, in the case of the CN and MN impersonation and of the MN reset, the device needs to send a PRes with about the same speed as the CN it replaces. It is not possible with our software on a computer, due to the slowness of an all-purpose non real-time operating system and of the network interface, when compared to B&R's optimized bus controller. It would be however possible to achieve even these attacks by using specific equipment, like an ASIC.

We consequently used a second testbed to complete our proof of concept. We used the OpenPOWERLINK software, a very advanced Ethernet POWERLINK implementation developed by the EPSG and fully compatible with the other devices of our testbed. This software is used to implement an MN on a computer. The CN is still the B&R's bus controller.

## 5.2   Results and Evaluation

**Denial of Service.** This attack is the simpler to test, and the results are the same on both testbeds. In those configurations, the minimal amount of SoC to send to cut the communications between the MN and the CN is two. The behavior of the system will be the same for a greater number of SoC. When the attack is over, the MN is still in the *operational* state, while the CN returns to the *pre_operational_1* state. The MN will consequently continue to send PReq to the CN. When it receives in the corresponding PRes that the CN is not in *operational* state anymore, the MN restarts. In the case of the first testbed, the application does not start correctly, and the CPU indicates that there was an error. If we connect it to the programming software to read the logbook, it signals the error "Module removed while running".

**ASnd Message Insertion.** We tested this attack on both testbeds to stop a CN. After we receive a void SoA, we send the NMT stop command. This attack

---

[1] http://www.br-automation.com/.

worked perfectly if the asynchronous period is long enough for us to be able to insert our frame (about 5 ms). We also tested for shorter cycle length with the first testbed. We always managed to have the command accepted, even in the shortest one possible (200 μs). The explanation is that, as we have only a CN, the isochronous period will always be short compared to the asynchronous period. In the case of a 200 μs cycle, we measured an isochronous period of 9.75 μs on average, with a maximum of 24 μs. In this worst case, we still have 88% of the cycle devoted to the asynchronous period, and therefore good odds to be able to send an ASnd in this time window.

When the CN is stopped, the MN still tries to poll data from it. After a few cycles without answer (the number depends of the MN configuration, 5 in our case), the MN restarts. As for the previous attack, in the case of the first testbed, the CPU restarts with an error.

**CN Impersonation.** This attack was only achieved in the second testbed, because with the first one, we are not quick enough to answer to the PReq frame. As this step is necessary for the MN reset attack and the MN impersonation attack, we will also only be able to perform those on the second testbed.

After the insertion of an NMT stop command to a CN with the previous attack, we were able to impersonate the CN timeslots in both the isochronous and asynchronous periods. This way, we could control the data the CN is sending, and affect the application. If we quit the impersonation of the CN, as when we stop the CN, the MN will restart after a few cycles. It is possible to release the CN from the *stopped* state by sending it a NMT-Enter-Pre-Operational-2 command (see Fig. 2). However, in the next cycle, the MN will see during the PReq/PRes exchange that the CN is not in the *operational* state. We tried to also send a NMT-Enable-Ready-to-Operate and NMT-Start-Node in the same asynchronous period, but it seems that only one change of state is possible per cycle. Sending directly an NMT-Start-Node does not work either.

**MN Reset and MN Impersonation.** We successfully stopped the MN and replaced it with another one, controlling consequently all the other devices.

## 6   Defense and Mitigation

### 6.1   Main Issues Detected

The attacks we presented in this paper are due to two main issues we found in the Ethernet POWERLINK protocol: the medium access control system by a Master/Slave paradigm, which implies that every device on the network will follow this rule, and the lack of authentication or basic verification in the asynchronous period.

The former issue leads to a trivial Denial of Service attack which cannot be avoided: the protocol was designed so that every device on a network would receive most of the traffic, by the use of special hard-coded multicast MAC address common to all the CNs and to the MN. Besides, the network equipment used should be either hubs (recommended) or switch acting as repeater. The Ethernet POWERLINK extension High Availability [25] offers the possibility to do media redundancy; however, it was designed to protect against a cable or hub failure, and would need to be adapted to be truly efficient against an attack. As for now, every device including the MN is connected to two different media, conveying the same messages. An interesting feature though is the possibility to have two MNs on one network configured in the same way: one is active (AMN) while the other is on standby (SMN) and acts as a CN, while monitoring all the network traffic. When the SMN detects an AMN failure (absence of one cycle) it should become the new SMN without going through the NMT boot-up process. This way, all the CNs stay in *operational* state and the system can continue with only one cycle interruption. If we use such an architecture with one main MN being connected to both the control and process network, and another redundant MN being connected only to the former (or to another differently secured process network), we can protect against a Denial of Service attack in the scenario of a compromised PLC, by shutting it down when we detect the attack.

The second issue is easier to deal with, and we propose in the two next subsections modifications of the Ethernet POWERLINK DLL (Data Link Layer) state machine and NMT state machine.

## 6.2  DLL State Machine Modifications

First, the CN should only accept a "correct" ASnd frame, that is an ASnd whose sender address and type are matching those of the SoA. With the exception of Async-only CN (CN whose data is polled during the asynchronous period), most will be void in a normal traffic. With this measure, we ensure that a void SoA implies that a CN does not take into account any frame in the cycle. In the case of a very short asynchronous period (short MTU or no legacy Ethernet traffic), it could be impossible to send two ASnd in a row: with this measure only, we could stop most of our attacks. However, if an attacker has time enough to send an ASnd frame in the remaining time, he could still perform the attack. He should nonetheless wait for an SoA with the correct type and sender to do so.

To prevent even this case, the CN should only accept one ASnd frame maximum, whatever the type and sender. As an ASnd is sent to every CN (and to the MN) thanks to a special multicast MAC address, a CN will be able in all case to know the number of ASnd (we do not consider the case of a man-in-the middle as stated in Sect. 2.3). This way, an attacker needs to be quick enough to send an ASnd before the normal sender; it becomes a race condition, possible only in some cases, as if the target is too close of the normal sender, an attacker trying to send an ASnd after an SoA would cause a collision.

We therefore propose to also modify the MN DLL state machine. As for a CN, it will only process the first "correct" ASnd frame. Most of the errors of Ethernet POWERLINK are handled for diagnosis with an item in the object dictionary which contains two types of counter and a threshold: a cumulative counter which is incremented at every occurrence of the error, and threshold counter, which is incremented by 8 at every cycle with an error, and decremented by one after an error-free cycle. Whenever this counter is higher than the threshold, the CN NMT state machine goes back to the *pre_operational_1* state. We propose to add such an item to the object dictionary with a new type of error: ASnd error. This error implies there might be an attack going on, with a small probability that a race condition might have been successful.

Figure 4 shows the normal (on the left) and the modified (on the right) DLL state machine of both an MN (on the top) and a CN (on the bottom). All the modifications we propose are shown in gray boxes. The transaction are represented as "event" → "reaction". An optional reaction is represented in square brackets. In both CN DLL state machines, an event which does not involve an error is written in bold.

### 6.3    NMT State Machine Modifications

When the ASnd error counter, defined in the previous subsection, goes over the defined threshold, we can think that it is not due to network error or unintended repetition, but due to an attack. In this case, an alarm is sent to the application (and, depending on the application, to an HMI). The MN will then reset

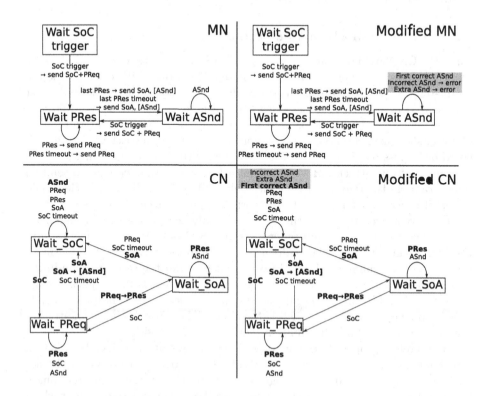

**Fig. 4.** DLL state machine modifications

all the CNs and go back to the *pre_operational_1* state. This will also happen in the *pre_operational_2* and *ready_to_operate* states where asynchronous communications are already started. The transition between *ready_to_operate* and *operational* only occurs if there is no error during a complete cycle like a collision, delay, lack of response from a CN, etc. If the MN detects an unwanted ASnd during this cycle, the MN should consider the cycle as incorrect.

Consequently, we are now able to detect when an attacker is trying to use the asynchronous period and to block it in most case. He might then have to try several times to be successful, but we would detect it either by collisions or ASnd errors. However, if an attacker succeeds the race condition in only a few tries, he can still be able to insert a command. We consider that the worst case is if an attacker is able to use an NMT command to stop a CN, as he will then be able to impersonate it. Besides, an NMT command always comes from the MN, so an unexpected ASnd of that type is necessarily an attack. We therefore add a transition in the MN NMT state machine which goes from any state after *pre_operational_2* to *pre_operational_1* if it receives an unexpected NMT command.

With these modifications, it is not possible anymore to impersonate a CN. Even if an attacker manages to send an NMT stop to the CN, the CN will be reset by the MN, leave the *stopped* state to go to the *pre_operational_1* state, and will then respond normally to the MN. In this case, as the MN sees two CNs with the same node id (the attacker and the CN), it will block the start-up phase. However, it is still possible, after a denial of service attack, to try to impersonate the MN by sending SoC frames when it is still in the *not_active* state. We therefore need to authenticate the MN. With the other modifications, we protect against MN impersonation from the *pre_operational_2* state. After that, any of our attack will take the MN to the *pre_operational_1*. The MN should consequently be authenticated between these two states, which will only slow down the start-up phase.

Figure 5 indicates both the normal (on the left) and modified (on the right) NMT state machines. Our modifications are in gray boxes.

## 6.4   Consequences on the System

The modifications of the DLL state machine are very light. No nodes have been added, and only a transition has been modified.

In term of memory, a device (CN or MN) need to be able to remember if the number of ASnd of the asynchronous period, i.e. 0 or 1. It can be done with only a bit. If the target specified in the SoA is $0 \times 00$ (no ASnd in the asynchronous period) or the node number of the device, it is put to 1; else to 0. When the CN receives an ASnd, it checks this value. If it is 1 it drops the frame. If it is 0, it consumes it normally. Only the MAC address is needed to know if it is an ASnd, so the CN just needs to read the 6 first bytes.

An MN should also have one additional object in its object dictionary. The error mechanism is the same as the other errors it can handle. Besides, the NMT state machine has two extra transitions to the *pre_operational_1* state

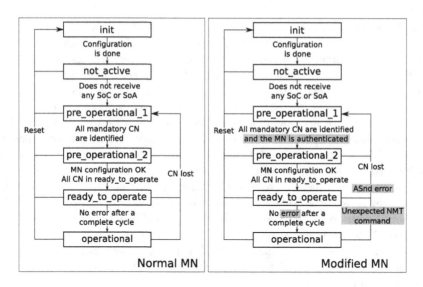

**Fig. 5.** NMT state machine modifications

when the ASnd error counter is higher than the threshold and when it receives an unexpected NMT command. In the first case, it means that in several cycles, there were too much ASnd. If it is not an attack, it implies that there was a few accidental insertions, which might be due to badly working equipment, unwanted delay or other network errors which could anyway lead to safety issues and would be detected by other error markers as collision detection, frame loss, etc. This does consequently not add any false positive. In the second case, an NMT command to a mandatory CN for a *stop*, *reset-node*, *enter-pre-operational-2*, etc. would have lead anyway in normal operating to the deactivation of a mandatory node, and therefore to put the MN in the *pre_operational_1* state. This additional mechanism only treats the special case not described in the specifications where someone stops a CN and immediately takes its slots.

Finally, the authentication mechanism is the only one adding major memory and computing constraints to the system. It would imply, for example, the possibility to exchange and stock symmetric keys on both MN and CNs, to compute a challenge or authentication octets like a MAC. However, this is done only during the start-up phase, and does not put constraints on the length of a cycle, which is the major issue in this case. Besides, as it is only used at the start-up of the system, this should rarely occur. Light and simple systems like a one-time pad could be used, with only constraints on memory on how many times we want to be able to boot the system up.

Consequently, our modifications barely impacts normal communications in *operational* state, and only slow down the start-up phase. It can be done by only changing the protocol and without modifying any equipment hardware.

# 7  Conclusion

Our analysis of the Ethernet POWERLINK protocol led to the implementation of several attacks, resulting in a loss of availability, or to the theft of the communication slots of a CN without causing any errors or, even more critical, of an MN and consequently of all the network. It is however possible to apply simple modifications to the state machines of a CN or of a MN to protect against most of these attacks. Defending the start-up phase of the MN is also crucial, as we do not protect against a restart of the system with a denial of service attack. We proposed to add a step of authentication in this phase; however, we only gave a few propositions on how to realize it. Some issues are still raised, including the way to exchange the information necessary to achieve this step (e.g. keys, algorithm). Future work could include a detail on this authentication during start-up, but also regularly during the cycle. An example of an authentication during runtime would be before an NMT command, or before the reading or writing of an item of the object dictionary; several levels of privilege could be implemented this way. The asynchronous period could be used to achieve it without extending the cycle time. The attacks in this paper also showed that the authentication of a CN can also be an issue, especially those of the sensors, which provide information to the system, and have consequently a certain amount of control on it.

# References

1. Neumann, P.: Communication in industrial automation what is going on? Contr. Eng. Pract. **15**, 1332–1347 (2007)
2. Jasperneite, J., Schumacher, M., Weber, K.: Limits of increasing the performance of industrial ethernet protocols. In: IEEE Conference on Emerging Technologies and Factory Automation (ETFA), pp. 17–24. IEEE (2007)
3. Ethernet POWERLINK Standardization Group: EPSG Draft Standard 301. Ethernet POWERLINK Communication Profile Specification (2013)
4. CAN in Automation: CiA 301 CANopen application layer specification (2011)
5. Falliere, N., Murchu, L.O., Chien, E.: W32. stuxnet dossier. White paper, Symantec Corp., Security Response 5 (2011)
6. Spenneberg, R., Brüggemann, M., Schwartke, H.: PLC-blaster: a worm living solely in the PLC (2016)
7. Huitsing, P., Chandia, R., Papa, M., Shenoi, S.: Attack taxonomies for the modbus protocols. Int. J. Crit. Infrastruct. Protect. **1**, 37–44 (2008)
8. Bristow, M.: Modscan: a scada modbus network scanner. In: DefCon-16 Conference, Las Vegas, NV (2008)
9. Spyridopoulos, T., Topa, I.-A., Tryfonas, T., Karyda, M.: A holistic approach for cyber assurance of critical infrastructure with the viable system model. In: Cuppens-Boulahia, N., Cuppens, F., Jajodia, S., Abou El Kalam, A., Sans, T. (eds.) SEC 2014. IAICT, vol. 428, pp. 438–445. Springer, Heidelberg (2014). doi:10.1007/978-3-642-55415-5_37
10. Antonioli, D., Tippenhauer, N.O.: Minicps: a toolkit for security research on CPS networks. In: Proceedings of the First ACM Workshop on Cyber-Physical Systems-Security and/or Privacy, pp. 91–100.1 ACM (2015)

11. Åkerberg, J., Björkman, M.: Exploring security in profinet IO. In: 33rd Annual IEEE International Computer Software and Applications Conference (COMPSAC 2009), vol. 1, pp. 406–412. IEEE (2009)

12. Paul, A., Schuster, F., König, H.: Towards the protection of industrial control systems – conclusions of a vulnerability analysis of profinet IO. In: Rieck, K., Stewin, P., Seifert, J.-P. (eds.) DIMVA 2013. LNCS, vol. 7967, pp. 160–176. Springer, Heidelberg (2013). doi:10.1007/978-3-642-39235-1_10

13. Bhatia, S., Kush, N., Djamaludin, C., Akande, J., Foo, E.: Practical modbus flooding attack and detection. In: Proceedings of the Twelfth Australasian Information Security Conference, vol. 149, pp. 57–65. Australian Computer Society, Inc. (2014)

14. Basecamp Digital Bond: Attacking ControlLogix: ControlLogix Vulnerability Report (2012)

15. Patel, S.C.: Secure Internet-Based Communication Protocol for SCADA Networks. University of Louisville (2006)

16. International Electrotechnical Commission: AGA Report No. 12. Cryptographic Protection of SCADA Communications Part 1: Background, Policies and Test Plan (2006)

17. West, A.: Securing DNP3 and modbus with AGA12-2J. In: 2008 IEEE Power and Energy Society General Meeting-Conversion and Delivery of Electrical Energy in the 21st Century, pp. 1–4. IEEE (2008)

18. Tsang, P.P., Smith, S.W.: YASIR: a low-latency, high-integrity security retrofit for legacy SCADA systems. In: Jajodia, S., Samarati, P., Cimato, S. (eds.) SEC 2008. ITIFIP, vol. 278, pp. 445–459. Springer, Boston, MA (2008). doi:10.1007/978-0-387-09699-5_29

19. Shahzad, A., Musa, S., Aborujilah, A., Irfan, M.: Secure cryptography testbed implementation for scada protocols security. In: 2013 International Conference on Advanced Computer Science Applications and Technologies (ACSAT), pp. 315–320. IEEE (2013)

20. Fovino, I.N., Carcano, A., Masera, M., Trombetta, A.: Design and implementation of a secure modbus protocol. In: Palmer, C., Shenoi, S. (eds.) ICCIP 2009. IAICT, vol. 311, pp. 83–96. Springer, Heidelberg (2009). doi:10.1007/978-3-642-04798-5_6

21. Hayes, G., El-Khatib, K.: Securing modbus transactions using hash-based message authentication codes and stream transmission control protocol. In: 2013 Third International Conference on Communications and Information Technology (ICCIT), pp. 179–184. IEEE (2013)

22. Wang, Y.: sSCADA: securing scada infrastructure communications. Int. J. Commun. Netw. Distrib. Syst. **6**, 59–78 (2010)

23. Czybik, B., Hausmann, S., Heiss, S., Jasperneite, J.: Performance evaluation of MAC algorithms for real-time ethernet communication systems. In: 2013 11th IEEE International Conference on Industrial Informatics (INDIN), pp. 676–681. IEEE (2013)

24. IEEE Power, Energy Society: IEEE 1815. IEEE Standard for Electric Power Systems Communications - Distributed Network Protocol (DNP3) (2012)

25. Ethernet POWERLINK Standardization Group: EPSG Draft Standard Proposal 302-A. Ethernet POWERLINK Part A, High Availability (2013)

# Secure Communication and Authentication Against Off-line Dictionary Attacks in Smart Grid Systems

Yongge Wang[✉]

UNC Charlotte, Charlotte, NC 28223, USA
yongge.wang@uncc.edu

**Abstract.** This paper studies the security requirements for remote authentication and communication in smart grid systems. Though smart card based authentication techniques have been a successful solution for addressing key management challenges in several cryptographic authentication systems, they may not be applicable to smart grid systems. For example, in order to unlock the credentials stored in tamper-resistant components (which could either be integrated in smart meters and collectors or be separate components that could be inserted into smart meters and collectors), one generally needs to input a password or PIN number to the smart meters or collectors. Since most smart meters and collectors are unattended, they could be maliciously modified or impersonated. Thus there is no trusted platform for the device owners or service provider agents to input the PIN number. Furthermore, the tamper resistant components (either integrated or separated) that hold the secret credentials could be easily accessed by an attacker and offline dictionary attacks could be easily mounted against these devices to retrieve the password or PIN number. In this paper, we review the security requirements for smart grid authentication systems and propose trust models for smart grid remote authentication systems. Finally, we propose secure authentication protocols within these trust models to defeat the common attacks such as offline dictionary attacks.

**Keywords:** Password authentication · Off-line attacks · Smart grid authentication

## 1 Introduction

The smart grid is a secure and intelligent energy distribution system that delivers energy from suppliers to consumers based on two-way demand and response digital communication technologies to control appliances at consumers' homes to save energy and increase reliability. The smart grid improves existing energy distribution systems with digital information management and advanced metering systems. Increased interconnectivity and automation over the grid systems presents new challenges for deployment and management.

© Springer International Publishing AG 2017
N. Cuppens-Boulahia et al. (Eds.): CyberICPS 2016, LNCS 10166, pp. 103–120, 2017.
DOI: 10.1007/978-3-319-61437-3_7

During 2011.02, more than 9,200 electric generating plants produced 312,334,000 megawatt-hours of electricity in the United States. Transmission lines distributed electricity to consumers in a 300,000 mile area. This power infrastructure was designed for performance and the integrated communications protocols were designed for bandwidth efficiency. However, cyber security was a low priority in the existing design of the power infrastructure systems. In order to transition from the current energy distribution infrastructure towards a smart grid, we have to overcome the challenges of integrating network-based security solutions with automation systems. Overcoming such challenges requires a combination of new and legacy components that may not have sufficient resources reserved to perform security functionalities (see, e.g., Wang [11,14]).

One of the challenges for securing smart grid systems is to counter attacks on advanced meter infrastructures (AMI). In order for smart grid systems to securely manage remotely located smart meters and collectors, each meter or collector should contain a unique identifying credential. A straightforward suggestion could be to assign a unique PKI certificate for each meter and each collector. However, a careful analysis shows that this is infeasible in many scenarios. For instance, collectors are generally mounted in unattended areas and smart meters are generally mounted outside of consumers' houses (for various reasons). Thus both internal and external attackers have easy access to these devices and may try to recover the credentials stored in these devices. In order to address these challenges, secure credentials must be stored in tamper resistant components and these components could either be integrated into meters and collectors or be separated tokens that could be inserted into meters and collectors. Under this new application scenario, traditional cryptographic protocols may be easily broken (some examples will be presented in the next paragraphs and sections) and new protocols should be designed.

The tamper resistant components for smart meters and collectors could either be integrated into meter and collector design or could be separate tokens that are held by service provider agents. There are different security implications for different designs and different security models are needed correspondingly. It is also a common practice for an agent (or owner) to input passwords or PIN numbers to unlock the credentials stored in the tamper resistant components during a secure communication or authentication session. In the case that the tamper resistant component is a separate design (tokens), they look more like smart cards and secure smart card based protocols that have discussed in the literature may be applicable (see, e.g., Wang [12]) in the smart grid systems. In particular, in these models, the smart meters and collectors could be malicious and should not be considered as trusted platforms in the design. One of the major challenges in such kind of system design is that the PIN number or password for unlocking the credential in tamper resistant storage system may be recovered using offline dictionary attacks efficiently.

Numerous smart card based cryptographic protocols rely on passwords selected by users (people) for strong authentication. Since the users find it inconvenient to remember long passwords, they typically select short easily-rememberable passwords. In these cases, the sample space of passwords may be small enough to be enumerated by an adversary thereby making the protocols vulnerable to a *dictionary* attack. It is desirable then to design password-based protocols that resist off-line dictionary attacks (see, e.g., [17]).

The problem of password-based remote authentication protocols was first studied by Gong, Lomas, Needham, and Saltzer [3] who used public-key encryption to guard against off-line password-guessing attacks. In another very influential work (see, e.g., [17]), Bellovin and Merritt introduced Encrypted Key Exchange (EKE), which became the basis for many of the subsequent works in this area. These protocols include SPEKE and SRP (see, e.g., [17]). In models discussed in the above mentioned papers, we can assume that there is a trusted client computer for the user to input her passwords. In a smart grid authentication system, this assumption may no longer be true. The smart meters and collectors (which can be considered as smart card readers in certain scenarios) could be malicious and may intercept the user inputted passwords. Furthermore, a smart card could be stolen and the adversary may launch an off-line dictionary attack against the stolen smart card itself. Wang [12] has introduced several security trust models for smart card based remote authentication and designed secure protocols within these models. This paper will concentrate on the security trust models and protocols for smart grid systems.

In a practical deployment of smart grid based authentication systems, there may be other system requirements. For example, we may be required to use symmetric cipher based systems only or to use public key based systems. Furthermore, the system may also require that the server store some validation data for each user or the server do not store any validation (this can be considered as identity based systems). Furthermore, there may be other requirements such as user password expiration and changes.

There have been quite a number of papers dealing with smart card based remote authentications (see, e.g., [1,2,4,6,8,9,16]) and most of these papers present attacks on protocols in previous papers and propose new protocols without proper security justification (or even a security model). Recently, Wang [12] has carried out a systematic analysis on security models for smart card based remote authentication and designed several secure protocols within these models. In this paper, we will carry out similar systematic researches on security models for smart grid authentication systems.

## 2   Communication Channels in Smart Grid Systems

Figure 1 shows a typical deployment of Advanced Meter Infrastructure (AMI) systems, where the collector nodes accumulate data from advanced meters and then submit data to the headquarter computing systems. This is a typical data collection model in AMI systems and normally there is no direct physical communication channel between meters and headquarter computing servers. However, virtual secure communication channels could always be established between a meter and the headquarter servers when necessary as described in Fig. 1. Furthermore, each of the meters and collectors may contain slots for a service provider agent to insert a secure token such as a smart card to initiate a sequence of secure activities such as remote authentication, meter/collector configuration, or secure communication between the service provider agent and headquarter computing systems via the meter/collector.

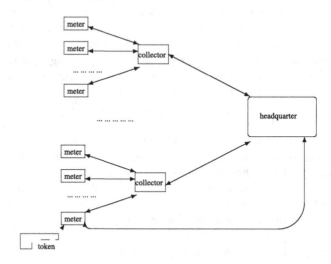

**Fig. 1.** A typical deployment of AMI systems

Though it is important to carry out research on general communication security and privacy preserving data collection in AMI systems, this paper concentrates on the following authenticated communication channels:

1. secure peer to peer authentication and communications among different nodes within the AMI systems. These nodes could be meters, collectors, or headquarters computing systems.
2. secure authentication of service provider agents or device owners via tokens (e.g., smart cards) inserted into meters and collectors.

It is common for one to ask whether it is possible to use existing techniques such as Kerberos and PKI that have been successfully used in Internet environments to secure the communications among meters, collectors, and headquarter computing systems. The answer to this question is that we have to be very careful in using existing techniques. In a smart grid system, meters and collectors are normally installed at unattended areas. Thus it may be easy for an attacker to get long time access to a large amount of meters and collectors without being detected. In order to deploy Kerberos and PKI based cryptographic systems in smart grid systems, each node must hold a secure key (either a secret key for a symmetric cipher or a private key for a public key system). If secret keys in meters and collectors are not appropriately protected, an attacker could easily obtain them. Tamper resistant techniques are typically used to protect these keys. In order to shorten our notations in following discussions, we will only mention smart meters unless stated otherwise. The discussion applies to collectors or separate tokens that could be inserted into meters or collectors as well.

We use an example to show the challenges in the design of secure smart grid based authentication protocols using tamper resistant techniques. A traditional way to store or transfer the secret key for each user is to use a symmetric key cipher such as AES to encrypt user's long term secret key with user's password and store the encrypted secret key in meters/collectors (either in integrated tamper resistant components of the meters/collectors or in separate tokens to be inserted into the nodes). This will not meet our security goals against off-line dictionary attacks. For example, in an RSA based public key cryptographic system, the public key is a pair of integers $(n, e)$ and the private key is an integer $d$. With the above mentioned traditional approach, the smart meter contains the value $AES_\alpha(d)$ in its tamper resistant memory space, where $\alpha$ is the user's password. If the adversary has access to the smart meter for certain time period, the adversary could feed a message (or challenge) $m$ to the smart meter for a signature. The adversary needs to input a password in order for the smart meter to generate a signature. The adversary will just pick one $\alpha'$ from her dictionary and ask the meter to sign $m$. The meter will "decrypt" the private key as $d' = AES_{\alpha'}^{-1}(AES_\alpha(d))$ and return a signature $s' = m^{d'} \bmod n$ on $m$. Then the adversary only needs to check whether $s'^e \bmod n = m$. If the equation holds, the adversary knows that the guessed password $\alpha'$ is correct. That is, $\alpha' = \alpha$. Otherwise, the attacker will remove $\alpha'$ from the dictionary. Similar attacks work for Guillou-Quisquater (GQ), Fiat-Shamir, and Schnorr zero-knowledge identification schemes.

This example shows that the "off-line" dictionary attack in the smart grid or AMI environments is different from the traditional client-server based off-line dictionary attacks. One potential approach to defeat this kind of attacks is to set a counter in the smart meter. That is, the smart meter is allowed to sign at most certain number of messages, and then self-destroy it. However, this kind of protection may not be feasible since the smart meters are normally deployed for a long time of services (e.g., 30 years) and it is hard to appropriately choose optimal values for the counter.

# 3    Security Models

First we provide a comprehensive list of attacks that a password-protected smart grid based authentication protocol needs to protect against. An ideal password-based authentication protocols for smart grid systems should be secure against these attacks and we will follow these criteria when we discuss the security of password-protected smart grid authentication protocols.

- **Eavesdropping**. The attacker may observe the communication channels.
- **Replay**. The attacker records messages (either from the communication channels between smart meters and service providers or between tamper resistant

components and non-tamper resistant components within the smart meters)
she has observed and re-sends them at a later time.

- **Man-in-the-middle.** The attacker intercepts the messages sent between the
  two parties (between user $\mathcal{U}$ and smart card $C$ or between smart card $C$ and
  servers $S$) and replaces these with her own messages. For example, if she sits
  between the user and the smart meter, then she could play the role of smart
  meter in the messages which it displays to the user on the smart meter and
  at the same time plays the role of users to the smart meter. A special man-
  in-the-middle attack is the *small subgroup attack*. We illustrate this kind of
  attack by a small example. Let $g$ be a generator of the group $G$ of order $n = qt$
  for some small $t > 1$. In a standard Diffie-Hellman key exchange protocol, the
  client $C$ chooses a random $x$ and sends $g^x$ to the server $S$, then $S$ chooses a
  random $y$ and sends $g^y$ to $C$. The shared key between $C$ and $S$ is $g^{xy}$. Now
  assume that the attacker $\mathcal{A}$ intercepts $C$'s message $g^x$, replaces it with $g^{xq}$,
  and sends it to $S$. $\mathcal{A}$ also intercepts $S$'s message $g^y$, replaces it with $g^{yq}$, and
  sends it to $C$. In the end, both $C$ and $S$ compute the shared key $g^{qxy}$. Since
  $g^{qxy}$ lies in the subgroup of order $t$ of the group generated by $g^q$, it takes on
  one of only $t$ possible values. $\mathcal{A}$ can easily recover this $g^{qxy}$ by an exhaustive
  search.

- **Impersonation.** The attacker impersonates the smart meter (using another
  smart meter that the attacker has access to or without using any smart
  meters) to authenticate to the remote service provider, impersonates a remote
  service provider to the smart meter, impersonates a token holder to the smart
  meter (if the smart grid is designed in such a way that a service provider agent
  uses some tokens to authenticate to smart meters) and a bogus smart meter
  impersonates an actual meter to a service provider agent with tokens.

- **Malicious smart meters.** The attacker controls the smart meter and intercepts a token holder inputted password. Furthermore, the attacker controls
  all of the communications between smart meter and the token holder, and
  all of the communications between smart meter and the remote server. For
  example, the attacker may launch a man in the middle attack between the
  token holder and the smart meter.

- **Stolen tokens.** The attacker steals a token from a service provider agent or
  an owner and impersonates the token holder to the remote server. In this case,
  the attacker could use the stolen token to impersonate the token holder with
  guessed passwords to the remote server with a limited time of failures since
  the server may disable the token from the server side after certain number of
  failures. If the attacker is allowed to use the token with guessed passwords
  to impersonate the token holder to the remote server for unlimited times of
  failures, then it will be considered as an on-line dictionary attack (a scenario
  that is not considered in this paper). However, the attacker is allowed for four
  kinds of further attacks that we will discuss in the following. One exception
  that we need to make in our security model is that we will not allow the
  attacker to control a malicious meter to intercept the token holder's password
  and then to steal the token from the token holder. There are four kinds of
  attackers based on the stolen token scenario:

- *Tamper resistant token with counter protection.* The attacker cannot read the sensitive information stored in the tamper resistant memory within the stolen token. Furthermore, the attacker may only issue a fixed amount of queries to the token to learn useful information. The token will be self-destroyed if the query number exceeds certain threshold (e.g., the GSM SIM card V2 or later has this capability).
- *Tamper resistant token without counter protection.* The attacker cannot read the sensitive information stored in the tamper resistant memory of th token. However, the attacker may issue a large amount of queries to the token to learn some useful information. For example, the attacker may setup a fake server and uses a malicious smart meter to guess the potential password.
- *Token is not tamper resistant.* The attacker (with the token) may be able to break the tamper resistant protection of the token and read the sensitive information stored in the tamper resistant memory. In this case, the token looks more like a USB memory stick that stores the user credential with password protection. But still there is a difference here. In order for the user to use USB memory stick based credentials, the user needs the access to a trusted computer to carry out the authentication. However, one may assume that even if the token is not tamper resistant, it is not possible for a malicious smart meter to read the sensitive information on the token within a short time period (e.g., during the time that the token owner inserts the token into the meter for an authentication).
- *Returned stolen token.* The attacker may steal the token from a token holder and carry out some analysis (e.g., mount some attacks based on the stolen token) and then return the token to the token holder without being detected by the token holder (that is, the token holder is not aware of the fact that the token has been lost for a while). The second author would like to thank Mr. Ding Wang for some discussions on related topics (note that Mr. Ding Wang is one of the authors for paper Wang et al. [10]).

- **Password-guessing**. The attacker is assumed to have access to a relatively small dictionary of words that likely includes the secret password $\alpha$. In an *off-line attack*, the attacker records past communications and searches for a word in the dictionary that is consistent with the recorded communications or carry out interaction with a stolen token without frequent server involvement (the attacker may carry out one or two sessions with server involved and all other activities without server involvement). In an *on-line attack*, the attacker repeatedly picks a password from the dictionary and attempts to impersonate $\mathcal{U}$, $\mathcal{C}$, $\mathcal{U}$ and $\mathcal{C}$, or $\mathcal{S}$. If the impersonation fails, the attacker removes this password from the dictionary and tries again, using a different password.
- **Partition attack**. The attacker records past communications, then goes over the dictionary and deletes those words that are not consistent with the recorded communications from the dictionary. After several tries, the attacker's dictionary could become very small.

We now informally sketch the definition of six types of security models.

1. **Type I.** The attacker $\mathcal{A}$ is allowed to watch regular runs of the protocol between a smart meter $\mathcal{R}$ (could be under the control of $\mathcal{A}$) and the server $\mathcal{S}$, can actively communicate with $\mathcal{R}$ and $\mathcal{S}$ in replay, impersonation, and man-in-the-middle attacks, and can also actively control a smart meter when a token holder inserts the token and inputs her password. Furthermore, the attacker may steal the token (e.g., smart card) from the token holder (if this happens, we assume that the attacker has not observed the user password from the previous runs of protocols) and issue a large amount of queries to the token using a malicious meter. However, we assume that the token is tamper resistant and the attacker could not read the sensitive data from the token. A protocol is said to be *secure* in the presence of such an attacker if (i) whenever the server $\mathcal{S}$ accepts an authentication session with $\mathcal{R}$, it is the case that the actual user $\mathcal{U}$ did indeed insert her token into $\mathcal{R}$ and input the correct password in the authentication session; and (ii) whenever a smart meter together with a token accepts an authentication session with $\mathcal{S}$, it is the case that $\mathcal{S}$ did indeed participate in the authentication session and the user $\mathcal{U}$ did indeed input the correct password.
2. **Type II.** The capability of the attacker is the same as in the Type I model except that when the attacker steals the token, it can only issue a fixed number of queries to the token using a malicious smart meter. If the number of queries exceeds the threshold, the token will be self-destroyed.
3. **Type III.** The capability of the attacker is the same as in the Type I model except that when the attacker steals the token, it will be able to read all of the sensitive data out from the token. But we will also assume that when a token holder inserts the token into a malicious smart meter for a session of authentication, the smart meter should not be able to read the information stored in the tamper resistant section of the token. In other words, the token is not tamper resistant only when the attacker can hold the token for a relatively long period by herself. Another equivalent interpretation of this assumption is that the attacker may not be able to intercept the password via the smart meter and read the information stored in the token at the same time.
4. **Type I-r, II-r, II-r.** The capability of the attacker is the same as in the Type I or Type II or Type III models respectively except that we allow returned stolen tokens.

# 4   Secure Authentication and Key Agreement Protocols for Smart Grid Systems

## 4.1   Symmetric Key Based Scheme: SSCA

In this symmetric key based smart grid authentication scheme SSCA, the server should choose a master secret $\beta$ and protect it securely. Note that this master secret $\beta$ could be different for different users (tokens). The Setup phase is as follows:

- For each user with identity $C$ and password $\alpha$, the token maker (it knows the server's master secret $\beta$) sets the token secret key as $K = \mathcal{H}(\beta, C)$ and stores $\mathcal{K} = \mathcal{E}_\alpha(K)$ in the tamper resistant memory of the token, where $\mathcal{E}$ is a symmetric encryption algorithm such as AES and $\mathcal{H}$ is a hash algorithm such as SHA-2.

In the SSCA scheme, we assume that the token has the capability to generate unpredictable random numbers. There are several ways for token to do so. One of the typical approaches is to use hash algorithms and EPROM. In this approach, a random number is stored in the EPROM of the smart card when it is made. Each time, when a new random number is needed, the token reads the current random number in the EPROM and hash this random number with a secret key. Then it outputs this keyed hash output as the new random number and replace the random number content in the EPROM with this new value. In order to keep protocol security, it is important for the token to erase all session information after each protocol run. This will ensure that, in case the token is lost and the information within the tamper resistant memory is recovered by the attacker, the attacker should not able to recover any of the random numbers used in the previous runs of the protocols. It should be noted that one may also use symmetric encryption algorithms to generate random numbers. Due to the reversible operation of symmetric ciphers, symmetric key based random number generation is not recommended for token implementation.

Each time when the user inserts her token into a meter (which could be malicious), the meter asks the user to input the password which will be forwarded to the token.

1. Using the provided password $\alpha$, the token decrypts $K = \mathcal{D}_\alpha(\mathcal{K})$. If the password is correct, the value should equal to $\mathcal{H}(\beta, C)$. The token selects a random number $R_c$, computes $R_A = \mathcal{E}_K(C, R_c)$, and sends the pair $(C, R_A)$ to the meter which will be forwarded to the server.

2. The server recovers the value of $(C, R_c)$ using the key $K = \mathcal{H}(\beta, C)$ and verifies that the identity $C$ of the token is correct. If the verification passes, the server selects a random number $R_s$, computes $R_B = \mathcal{E}_K(C, R_s)$, and sends $(C, R_B, C_s)$ to the meter which forwards it to the token. Here $C_s = \mathrm{HMAC}_{sk}(\mathcal{S}, C, R_s, R_c)$ is the keyed message authentication tag on $(\mathcal{S}, C, R_s, R_c)$ under the key $sk = \mathcal{H}(C, \mathcal{S}, R_c, R_s)$ and $\mathcal{S}$ is the server identity string.

3. The token recovers the value of $(C, R_s)$ using the key $K = \mathcal{H}(\beta, C)$, computes $sk = \mathcal{H}(C, \mathcal{S}, R_c, R_s)$, and verifies the HMAC authentication tag $C_s$. If the verification passes, it computes its own confirmation message as $C_c = \mathrm{HMAC}_{sk}(C, \mathcal{S}, R_c, R_s)$ and sends $C_c$ to the server. The shared session key will be $sk$.

4. The server accepts the communication if the HMAC tag $C_c$ passes the verification.

The protocol SSCA message flows are shown in the Fig. 2.

$$\underline{\text{Token}} \longrightarrow \underline{\text{Server}} : C, \mathcal{E}_K(C, R_c)$$
$$\underline{\text{Token}} \longleftarrow \underline{\text{Server}} : \mathcal{E}_K(C, R_s), C_s$$
$$\underline{\text{Token}} \longrightarrow \underline{\text{Server}} : C_c$$

**Fig. 2.** Message flows in SSCA

In the following, we use heuristics to show that SSCA is a secure authentication protocol in the Type I and Type II security models. If the underlying encryption scheme $\mathcal{E}$ and HMAC are secure, then eavesdropping, replay, man-in-the-middle, impersonation, password-guessing, and partition attacks will learn nothing about the password since no information of password is involved in these messages. Furthermore, a malicious meter can intercept the password, but without the token itself, the attacker will not be able to learn information about the secret key $K = \mathcal{D}_\alpha(\mathcal{K})$. Thus the attacker will not be able to impersonate the server or the token owner. When the attacker steals the token (but she has not controlled a meter to intercept the token owner password in the past), she may be able to insert the token into a malicious meter and let the token to run the protocols with a fake server polynomial many times. In these protocol runs, the attacker could input guessed password $\alpha'$. The token will output $(C, \mathcal{E}_{K'}(C, R_c))$ where $K' = \mathcal{D}_{\alpha'}(\mathcal{K})$. Since the attacker has no access to the actual server (this is an off-line attack), the attacker can not verify whether the output $(C, \mathcal{E}_{K'}(C, R_c))$ is in correct format. Thus the attacker has no way to verify whether the guessed password $\alpha'$ is correct. In a summary, the protocol is secure in the Type I and Type II security models.

The protocol SSCA is not secure in the Type III security model. Assume that the attacker has observed a previous valid run of the protocol (but did not see the password) before steals the token. For each guessed password $\alpha'$, the attacker computes a potential key $K' = \mathcal{D}_{\alpha'}(\mathcal{K})$. If this key $K'$ is not consistent with the observed confirmation messages in the previous run of the protocol, the attacker could remove $\alpha'$ from the password list. Otherwise, it guessed the correct password.

If we revise the attacker's capability in Type III model by restricting the attacker from observing any valid runs of the protocol before she steals the token, we get a new security model which we will call Type III' model. We can show that the protocol SSCA is secure in the Type III' model. The heuristics is that for an attacker with access to the value $\mathcal{K} = \mathcal{E}_\alpha(K)$, he will not be able to verify whether a guessed password is valid off-line. For example, for each guessed password $\alpha'$, she can compute $K' = \mathcal{D}_{\alpha'}(\mathcal{K})$. But she has no idea whether $K'$ is the valid secret key without on-line interaction with the server. Thus the protocol is secure in the Type III' security model.

**Remarks:** Modification of the protocol may be necessary for certain applications. For example, if the token identification string $C$ itself needs to be protected (e.g., it is the credit card number), then one certainly does not want to transfer the identification string $C$ along with the message in a clear channel.

## 4.2  Public Key Based Scheme: PSCAb

In this section, we introduce a public key based token authentication scheme with bilinear groups: PSCAb, it is based on the identity based key agreement protocol from IEEE 1363.3 [5,13].

In the following, we first briefly describe the bilinear maps and bilinear map groups.

1. $G$ and $G_1$ are two (multiplicative) cyclic groups of prime order $q$.
2. $g$ is a generator of $G$.
3. $\hat{e} : G \times G \to G_1$ is a bilinear map.

A bilinear map is a map $\hat{e} : G \times G \to G_1$ with the following properties:

1. bilinear: for all $g_1, g_2 \in G$, and $x, y \in Z$, we have $\hat{e}(g_1^x, g_2^y) = \hat{e}(g_1, g_2)^{xy}$.
2. non-degenerate: $\hat{e}(g, g) \neq 1$.

We say that $G$ is a bilinear group if the group action in $G$ can be computed efficiently and there exists a group $G_1$ and an efficiently computable bilinear map $\hat{e} : G \times G \to G_1$ as above. For convenience, throughout the paper, we view both $G$ and $G_1$ as multiplicative groups though the concrete implementation of $G$ could be additive elliptic curve groups.

Let $k$ be the security parameter given to the setup algorithm and $IG$ be a bilinear group parameter generator. We present the scheme by describing the three algorithms: **Setup**, **Extract**, and **Exchange**.

**Setup**: For the input $k \in Z^+$, the algorithm proceeds as follows:

1. Run $IG$ on $k$ to generate a bilinear group $G_\rho = \{G, G_1, \hat{e}\}$ and the prime order $q$ of the two groups $G$ and $G_1$. Choose a random generator $g \in G$.
2. Pick a random master secret $\beta \in Z_q^*$.
3. Choose cryptographic hash functions $\mathcal{H}_1 : \{0,1\}^* \to G$, $\mathcal{H}_2 : \{0,1\}^* \to \{0,1\}^*$, and $\pi : G \times G \to Z_q^*$. In the security analysis, we view $\mathcal{H}_1$, $\mathcal{H}_2$, and $\pi$ as random oracles.

The system parameter is $\langle q, g, G, G_1, \hat{e}, \mathcal{H}_1, \mathcal{H}_2, \pi \rangle$ and the master secret key is $\beta$.

**Extract**: For a given identification string $C \in \{0,1\}^*$, the algorithm computes a generator $g_C = \mathcal{H}_1(C) \in G$, and sets the private key $d_C = g_C^\beta$ where $\beta$ is the master secret key. The algorithm will further compute $g_S = \mathcal{H}_1(S) \in G$ where $S$ is the server identity string, and store value $(C, g_S, d_C')$ in the tamper resistant token where $d_C' = \mathcal{E}_{\mathcal{H}_2(\alpha)}(d_C)$, $\alpha$ is token owner's password. And $\mathcal{E}$ is the encryption function that could be defined in one of the following ways:

1. $\mathcal{E}$ is a standard symmetric cipher such as AES
2. $\mathcal{E}_{\mathcal{H}_2(\alpha)}(d_C) = \text{AES}_{\mathcal{H}_2(\alpha)}(d_C) + i_0$ where $i_0 = \min\{i : \text{AES}_{\mathcal{H}_2(\alpha)}(d_C) + i \in G, i = 0, 1, \ldots\}$. For an inputted password $\alpha'$, $d_C$ is computed as $\text{AES}_{\mathcal{H}_2(\alpha')}^{-1}(d_C' - i_0)$ where $i_0 = \min\{i : \text{AES}_{\mathcal{H}_2(\alpha')}^{-1}(d_C' - i) \in G, i = 0, 1, \ldots\}$.
3. $\mathcal{E}_{\mathcal{H}_2(\alpha)}(d_C) = d_C^{\mathcal{H}_2(\alpha)}$

**Exchange**: The algorithm proceeds as follows.

1. The token selects $x \in_R Z_q^*$, computes $R_A = g_C^x$, and sends it to the Server via the meter.
2. The Server selects $y \in_R Z_q^*$, computes $R_B = g_S^y$, and sends it to the token.
3. The token computes $s_A = \pi(R_A, R_B)$, $s_B = \pi(R_B, R_A)$, and $d_C = \mathcal{D}_{\mathcal{H}_2(\alpha')}(d_C')$ where $\mathcal{D}$ is the decryption function and $\alpha'$ is the user inputted password. If $d_C$ is not an element of $G$, the token chooses the value for $sk$ as a random element of $G_1$. Otherwise, the token computes the value $sk = \hat{e}(g_C, g_S)^{(x+s_A)(y+s_B)\beta}$ as

$$\hat{e}\left(d_C^{(x+s_A)}, g_S^{s_B} \cdot R_B\right).$$

4. The token computes $K_1 = \mathcal{H}(sk, R_A, R_B, C, S, 1)$, $K_2 = \mathcal{H}(sk, R_A, R_B, C, S, 2)$, and sends value $C_C = \mathrm{HMAC}_{K_1}(C, S, R_A, R_B)$ to the server. $K_2$ is the shared secret.
5. Server computes $s_A = \pi(R_A, R_B)$, $s_B = \pi(R_B, R_A)$ and $sk$ as

$$\hat{e}(g_C, g_S)^{(x+s_A)(y+s_B)\beta} = \hat{e}\left(g_C^{s_A} \cdot R_A, g_S^{(y+s_B)\beta}\right).$$

6. Server verifies whether $C_C$ is correct. If the verification passes, server computes $K_1 = \mathcal{H}(sk, , R_A, R_B, C, S, 1)$, $K_2 = \mathcal{H}(sk, , R_A, R_B, C, S, 2)$ and sends the value $C_S = \mathrm{HMAC}_{K_1}(S, C, R_B, R_A)$ to the token. $K_2$ is the shared secret.
7. The token verifies the value of $C_S$.

The token should never export the value of $sk$ to the meter during the protocol run. However, the token may need to export $K_2$ to the meter in certain applications.

The protocol PSCAb message flows are shown in the Fig. 3

$$\begin{aligned}
\text{Token} &\longrightarrow \text{Server} : g_C^x \\
\text{Token} &\longleftarrow \text{Server} : g_S^y \\
\text{Token} &\longrightarrow \text{Server} : C_C \\
\text{Token} &\longleftarrow \text{Server} : C_S
\end{aligned}$$

**Fig. 3.** Message flows in PSCAb

In the following, we use heuristics to show that PSCAb is secure in the Type I, Type II, and Type III security models. It should be noted that if the encryption function is chosen as a standard symmetric cipher such as AES, then PSCAb is only weakly secure in the Type III security model as follows. When the attacker has access to the value $d_C'$, she could remove those $\alpha'$ from her dictionary such that $\mathcal{D}_{\mathcal{H}_2(\alpha')}(d_C')$ is not an element of $G$. In other words, PSCAb is secure in the Type III security model only if the remaining dictionary is still large enough.

The security of the underlying identity based key agreement protocol WANG-KE [5,13] is proved in [13]. Furthermore, the eavesdropping, replay, man-in-the-middle, impersonation, password-guessing, and partition attacks will learn nothing about the password since no information of password is involved in these messages. Furthermore, these attackers will learn nothing about the private keys $d_C$ and $\beta$ based on the proofs in [13]. For an attacker with access to the information $d'_C$ (the attacker may read this information from the stolen token), she may impersonate the token owner to interact with the server. Since the attacker could not compute the correct value $sk$, she will not be able to generate the confirmation message $C_C$. Thus the server will not send the server confirmation message back to the attacker. In another word, the attacker will get no useful information for an off-line password guessing attack. Furthermore, even if the attacker has observed previous valid protocol runs, it will not help the attacker since the token does not contain any information of the session values $x$ of the previous protocols runs.

**Remarks:** In the protocol PSCAb, it is important to have the token to send the confirmation message to the server first. Otherwise, PSCAb will not be secure in the Type III security model. Assume that the server sends the first confirmation message. After the attacker obtains the value $d'_C$ from the token, she could impersonate the user by sending the vale $R_A$ to the server. After receiving the server confirmation message, she will remove $\alpha'$ from her dictionary such that

$$sk' = \hat{e}\left(\mathcal{D}_{\mathcal{H}(\alpha')}(d'_C)^{(x+s_A)}, g_S^{s_B} \cdot R_B\right)$$

is not consistent with the confirmation message $C_S$.

## 4.3   Public Key Based Scheme: PSCA

In the previous section, we presented a protocol PSCAb based on the identity based key agreement protocol WANG-KE. In this section, we briefly discuss a protocol based on the HMQV key agreement protocol [7]. Let $g$ be the generator of the group $G_\rho$, $q$ be the prime order of $g$, and $h$ be a constant. In this case, the server and the token will both have public keys.

The server private/public key pair is $(b, g^b)$. The token private/public key pair is $(a, g^a)$. The data stored on the token is: $(a \times \mathcal{H}(\alpha), g^b)$. In the following, we use $C$ and $S$ to denote the client (token) and server identity strings respectively.

1. The token selects $x \in_R [1, q-1]$, computes $R_A = g^x$, and sends it to the server.
2. Server selects $y \in_R [1, q-1]$, computes $R_B = g^y$, and sends it to the token.
3. The token decrypts the private key $a$ via the user inputted password, computes $\pi_A = \mathcal{H}(R_A, S)$, $\pi_B = \mathcal{H}(R_B, C)$, $s_A = (x + \pi_A a) \bmod q$, and the shared session key: $K_{\text{HMQV}} = (R_B \cdot (g^b)^{\pi_B})^{s_A h}$.
4. The server computes $\pi_A = \mathcal{H}(R_A, S)$, $\pi_B = \mathcal{H}(R_B, C)$, $s_B = (y + \pi_B b) \bmod q$, and the shared session key: $K_{\text{HMQV}} = (R_A \cdot (g^a)^{\pi_A})^{s_B h}$.

**Remarks**: Heuristics could be used to show that this protocol is secure in the Type I and Type II security models. However this protocol is not secure in the Type III security model. After the attacker obtains the value $(a \times \mathcal{H}(\alpha), g^b)$, the attacker could recover the password from $a \times \mathcal{H}(\alpha)$ and the token public key $g^a$. However, if $g^a$ is only known to the server, then PSCA should be secure in the Type III model. We conjecture that it may be impossible to design HMQV based protocols that are secure in the Type III model if the public key of the token is available to the attackers.

### 4.4 Public Key Based Scheme with Password Validation Data at Server: PSCAV

In previous sections, we discussed two protocols SSCA and PSCAb that the server does not store any password validation data. In this section, we discuss a protocol where the server needs to store password validation data for each token. One of the disadvantages of this kind of protocols is that if the token owner wants to change her password, the server has to be involved.

It should be noted that the password based remote authentication protocols that have been specified in the IEEE 1363.2 [5] are not secure in our models. The major reason is that the only secure credential that a client owns is the password. If the token owner inputs her password on an untrusted meter, the meter could just record the password and impersonates the client to the server without the token in future.

Before we present our scheme PSCAV, we briefly note that the protocol PSCAb in Sect. 4.2 can be easily modified to be a password protected token authentication scheme that the server stores user password validation data. In Sect. 4.2, the identity string for each user is computed as $g_C = \mathcal{H}(C) \in G$. For protocols with password validation data, we can use a different way to compute the identity strings. In particular, assume that the user $\mathcal{U}$ has a password $\alpha$, then the identity string for the user will be computed as $g_C = \mathcal{H}(C, \alpha) \in G$ and the private key for the user will be $d_C = g_C^\beta$ where $\beta$ is the master secret key. The value $(C, g_S, \mathcal{E}_{\mathcal{H}_2(\alpha)}(d_C))$ will be stored in the tamper resistant token, and the value $g_C$ will be stored in the server database for this user. The remaining protocol runs the same as in Sect. 4.2. We can call the above mentioned protocol as PSCAbV.

Now we begin to describe our main protocol PSCAV for this section. Assume that the server has a master secret $\beta$ ($\beta$ could be user specific also). For each user with password $\alpha$, let the user specific generator be $g_C = \mathcal{H}_1(C, \alpha, \beta)$, the value $g_C^{\mathcal{H}_2(\alpha)}$ is stored on the token, where $\mathcal{H}_2$ is another independent hash function. The value $g_C = \mathcal{H}_1(C, \alpha, \beta)$ will be stored in the server database for this user. The remaining of protocol runs as follows:

1. The token selects random $x$ and sends $R_A = g_C^x$ to the server.
2. Server selects random $y$ and sends $R_B = g_C^y$ to the token.
3. The token computes $u = \mathcal{H}(C, S, R_A, R_B)$ where $S$ is the server identity string, $sk = g_C^{y(x+u\alpha)}$, and sends $C_c = \mathcal{H}(sk, C, S, R_A, R_B, 1)$ to the server.

4. After verifying that $C_c$ is correct, server. computes $u = \mathcal{H}(C, \mathcal{S}, R_A, R_B)$, $sk = g_C^{y(x+u\alpha)}$, and sends the value $C_s = \mathcal{H}(sk, \mathcal{S}, C, R_B, R_A, 2)$ to the token.

The protocol PSCAV message flows are the same as for the PSCAb protocol message in the Fig. 3 (but with different interpretation for the variables in the figure).

In the following, we use heuristics to show that PSCAV is secure in the Type I, Type II, and Type III security models. For the PSCAV protocol, the eavesdropping, replay, man-in-the-middle, token (client) impersonation, password-guessing, and partition attacks will learn nothing about the password due to the hardness of the Diffie-Hellman problem. For the attacker that carries out a server impersonation attack, it will receive the value $R_A$, and send a random $R_B$ to the token. The attacker will then receive the token confirmation message $C_C$. The attacker may not launch an off-line dictionary attack on these information since for each guessed password $\alpha'$, it has no way to generate a session key $sk'$ due to the hardness of the Diffie-Hellman problem. For an attacker with access to the information $g_C^{\mathcal{H}_2(\alpha)}$ (the attacker may read this information from the stolen token), she may impersonate the token owner to interact with the server. The attacker may send a random $R_A$ to the server which could be based on $g_C^{\mathcal{H}_2(\alpha)}$, and receives a value $R_B$ from the server. But it cannot compute the correct value for $sk$ based on these information. Thus it could not send the confirmation message $C_C$ to the server. Thus the server will not send the server confirmation message back to the attacker. In other words, the attacker will get no useful information for an off-line password guessing attack. Furthermore, even if the attacker has observed previous valid protocol runs, it will not help the attacker since the token does not contain any information of the session values $x$ of the previous protocols runs.

**Remarks**: The attack described in the Remarks at the end of Sect. 4.2 could be used to show that it is important to have the token to send the confirmation message to the server first in the protocol PSCAV also.

## 5   Peer to Peer Communication in Smart Grid Systems

In the previous sections, we presented smart grid authentication and communication protocols in the client-server model. In advanced smart grid systems, peer to peer communications among meters and collectors are essential also. In this section, we present a yellow page protocol for peer to peer authentication and communication in smart grid systems.

PKI and Kerberos systems are extensively used in Internet environments for peer to peer authentication and communication. However, Kerberos requires an online trusted server for 24 h a day and PKI requires updated CRL (certificate revocation list) in real time. It is generally very expensive to maintain these services with guaranteed security. Since nodes of smart grid systems are relatively stable for a given period of time, we may design secure authentication and communication protocols based on yellow page services (e.g., LDAP servers).

A yellow page service (e.g., LDAP server) is generally read-only and easy to maintain.

In the Yellow Page protocol YP, each node $A$ has a secret key $K_A$ which is stored in the tamper resistant component of node $A$ (could be contained in a separate token such as smart card) and there is an online yellow page $Y$ that stores the following entry for each ordered node pair $\langle A, B \rangle$ of the AMI system:

$$\langle A, B \rangle : \mathcal{E}_{K_A}(\mathcal{H}(K_B, A), B, A).$$

Note that $K_A$ should be a random key with sufficient entropy and it could be protected with memorable password within the tamper resistant component of node $A$. If $K_A$ does not have sufficient entropy, then off-line dictionary attacks are possible against the Yellow page protocol.

Each time when a node $A$ wants to talk to a node $B$, the participating parties follow the following steps of the protocol:

1. $A$ retrieves from the Yellow Page $Y$ the entry $\langle A, B \rangle : \mathcal{E}_{K_A}(\mathcal{H}(K_B, A), B, A)$, and decrypts $\tau = \mathcal{H}(K_B, A)$.
2. $A$ chooses a random value $r$ and sends it to $B$.
3. $B$ chooses a random value $s$ and sends the following pair $(s, \mathcal{H}'(\mathcal{H}(K_B, A), r, s, 0))$ to $A$.
4. After receiving $(s, \sigma)$ from $B$, $A$ checks whether $\sigma = \mathcal{H}'(\tau, r, s, 0)$, and sends $\delta = \mathcal{H}'(\tau, s, 1)$ to Bob.
5. $B$ checks whether $\delta = \mathcal{H}'(\mathcal{H}(K_B, A), s, 1)$.

The session key for nodes $A$ and $B$ to carry out subsequence communications is computed as $sk = \mathcal{H}'(\tau, s, A, B)$.

The full message flow for the yellow page protocol YP are shown in the Fig. 4.

$$\underline{A} \longleftarrow \underline{Y} : \mathcal{E}_{K_A}(\mathcal{H}(K_B, A), B, A)$$
$$\underline{A} \longrightarrow \underline{B} : r$$
$$\underline{A} \longleftarrow \underline{B} : (s, \mathcal{H}'(\mathcal{H}(K_B, A), r, s, 0))$$
$$\underline{A} \longrightarrow \underline{B} : \mathcal{H}'(\tau, s, 1)$$

**Fig. 4.** Message flow in YP

### 5.1  A Note on a Paper Appeared in IEEE Transaction on Smart Grid

It is always challenging to design secure authentication protocols appropriately. A student of the author of this paper published a paper [15] in the IEEE Transactions on Smart Grid without getting permission from Dr. Wang and included Dr. Wang as the co-author in that paper [15]. In this section, we briefly show that the protocol presented in [15] could be trivially broken.

In the "secure communication protocol" presented in [15], there is one trusted center $T$ and several users (smart meters). Each user has a password. When Alice wants to talk to Bob, they will carry out the following protocol (note that both Alice and Bob could be smart meters or service provider stations):

- Alice sends "(Alice, Bob)" to $T$, Alice chooses a random $r$ and sends "$(r,$ Alice)" to Bob.
- $T$ computes $\varepsilon = ENC(K_{alice}, \mathcal{H}(K_{bob}, Alice))$ and sends it to Alice, where $ENC$ is a symmetric encryption scheme and $K_{alice}$ and $K_{bob}$ are Alice and Bob's passwords respectively.
- After Bob receives $r$ from Alice, Bob chooses a random $s$ and sends the value $(s, \sigma = \mathcal{H}'(\mathcal{H}(K_{bob}, Alice), r, s, 0))$ to Alice.
- Bob computes the session key

$$sk = \mathcal{H}'(\mathcal{H}(K_{Bob}, Alice), s, Alice, Bob)$$

- Alice decrypts

$$token = DEC(K_{alice}, \varepsilon) = \mathcal{H}(K_{bob}, Alice),$$

checks that $\sigma = \mathcal{H}'(token, r, s, 0)$, and sends the value $\delta = \mathcal{H}'(token, s, 1)$ to Bob
- Bob checks whether $\delta = \mathcal{H}'(\mathcal{H}(K_{bob}, Alice), s, 1)$.

In the following, we present a trivial attack on the above protocol. Our attacks show that Carol can talk to Alice pretending to be Bob and Alice believes that she is talking to Bob though she is talking to Carol. In particular, the adversary Carol carries out the following steps of the attack:

- When Alice wants to talk to Bob, Alice sends the value "(Bob, Alice)" to $T$. At this stage, the adversary Carol intercepts this message and changes it to "(Carol, Alice)". $T$ will reply $ENC(K_{Alice}, \mathcal{H}(K_{carol}, Alice))$ and Carol will forward this to Alice
- Alice sends "$(r, Alice)$" to Bob. Bob will not get this message though Carol (impersonating Bob) will get it.
- Carol (impersonating Bob) sends the value

$$(s, \mathcal{H}'(\mathcal{H}(K_{carol}, Alice), r, s, 0))$$

to Alice
- Alice sends $\mathcal{H}(token, s, 1)$ to Carol (impersonating Bob).

Now Alice is talking to Carol though Alice thinks that she is talking to Bob.

# References

1. Chen, Y., Chou, J., Huang, C.: Comment on four two-party authentication protocols (2010)
2. Das, M.L., Saxena, A., Gulati, V.P.: A dynamic ID-based remote user authentication scheme. IEEE Trans. Consum. Electron. **50**, 629–631 (2004)
3. Gong, L., Lomas, M.A., Roger, M., Needham, R.M., Saltzer, J.H.: Protecting poorly chosen secrets from guessing attacks. IEEE J. Sel. Areas Commun. **11**, 648–656 (1993)
4. Goriparthi, T., Das, M.L., Saxena, A.: An improved bilinear pairing based remote user authentication scheme. Comput. Stand. Interfaces **31**, 181–185 (2009)
5. IEEE 1363: Standard specifications for public-key cryptography (2005)
6. Juang, W.S., Chen, S.T., Liaw, H.T.: Robust and efficient password-authenticated key agreement using smart cards. IEEE Trans. Ind. Electron. **55**, 2551–2556 (2008)
7. Krawczyk, H.: HMQV: a high-performance secure Diffie-Hellman protocol. Cryptology ePrint Archive, Report 2005/176 (2005). http://eprint.iacr.org/
8. Lee, Y., Nam, J., Won, D.: Vulnerabilities in a remote agent authentication scheme using smart cards. In: Nguyen, N.T., Jo, G.S., Howlett, R.J., Jain, L.C. (eds.) KES-AMSTA 2008. LNCS, vol. 4953, pp. 850–857. Springer, Heidelberg (2008). doi:10.1007/978-3-540-78582-8_86
9. Rhee, H.S., Kwon, J.O., Lee, D.H.: A remote user authentication scheme without using smart cards. Comput. Stand. Interfaces **31**, 6–13 (2009)
10. Wang, D., Ma, C.: Robust smart card based password authentication scheme against smart card security breach. Technical report, Cryptology ePrint Archive, Report 2012/439 (2012). http://eprint.iacr.org/2012/439
11. Wang, Y.: Cryptographic challenges in smart grid system security. In: IEEE Smart Grid News Letters, December 2012. http://smartgrid.ieee.org/december-2012/732-cryptographic-challenges-in-smart-grid-system-security
12. Wang, Y.: Password protected smart card and memory stick authentication against off-line dictionary attacks. In: Gritzalis, D., Furnell, S., Theoharidou, M. (eds.) SEC 2012. IAICT, vol. 376, pp. 489–500. Springer, Heidelberg (2012). doi:10.1007/978-3-642-30436-1_40
13. Wang, Y.: Efficient identity-based and authenticated key agreement protocol. Trans. Comput. Sci. **17**, 172–197 (2013)
14. Wang, Y.: Smart grid, automation, and SCADA systems security. In: Xiao, Y. (ed.) Security and Privacy in Smart Grids, pp. 245–268. CRC Press, July 2013
15. Xia, J., Wang, Y.: Secure key distribution for the smart grid. IEEE Trans. Smart Grid **3**(3), 1437–1443 (2012)
16. Xiang, T., Wong, K., Liao, X.: Cryptanalysis of a password authentication scheme over insecure networks. Comput. Syst. Sci. **74**, 657–661 (2008)
17. Zhao, Z., Dong, Z., Wang, Y.: Security analysis of a password-based authentication protocol proposed to IEEE 1363. Theor. Comput. Sci. **352**, 280–287 (2006)

# Author Index

Printed in the United States
By Bookmasters